The
KINGDOM
of GOD

Our Life with Jesus the King

JOHN AVERY

THE SPARKS SERIES

THE SPARKS SERIES

ISBN: 978-0-9986507-6-0 (Paperback)
ISBN: 978-0-9986507-7-7 (eBook)

Cover design by Nada Orlic
Formatting by Luca Funari

Cover image: LoveTheWind

Many of the pieces in this collection first appeared on *www.BibleMaturity.com*.

CONTENTS

The
SPARKS SERIES

The pieces I write are not exactly devotionals though they have some of the flavor of a devotional: they are short enough to be read in a few minutes and can be used daily for a few weeks, each is a reflection on at least one Bible verse, and some life application is encouraged. However, the pieces are designed to stimulate deeper reflection than the average devotional. I think of them as sparks.

Jesus' life and words frequently challenged people's established ways of living. He didn't come to bless life as we know it; He invites us to lay down our old ways and receive His kingdom life instead. When a wildfire rages through brush, it quickly consumes the dead and the dry. After the rain, and the space of a few weeks, new life sprouts. I pray that these pieces will be sparks to lives that are surrendered to burning and committed to the slower process of nurturing kingdom ways in place of the old.

My prayer is that a flame would ignite in your brain, fire up your thinking, race to your heart, and jump from the tips of your fingers, toes, and tongue. Feed the flames so that your thoughts turn to passion, and your passion to action. May it be of such intensity that, everywhere you walk, every life that you touch glows brightly in turn.

No fire has value except the fire of the glory of God. The words of the Bible are more important than mine. For the sake of space, I have only included a few verses in each piece (noted on the Contents page). So, please take time to reflect on each Scripture in its context and, if possible, read any parallel accounts (provided under chapter headings). Imagine the scenes and consider the characters. As I read the passages, the Spirit's finger pointed at things in my life and inspired each piece; ask Him to work in your life too. It's His finger that beckons us out of our old ways and points us to the ways of Jesus.

May you burn with His fire as a result of reflecting on these simple sparks.

Look out for other compilations of short pieces on topics like:

- *The Questions of Jesus* — Published October 2022
- Our Identity as Children of God
- Conversation with God (commonly called prayer)
- Faith in God
- The Spirit of God
- Following the Voice of God (calling and guidance)
- Revival from God
- Prophets of God
- Names of God
- Followers of Jesus (what it means to be a disciple)
- Kings of Israel (David, Saul, and others)
- Fathers of Faith (Abraham, Jacob, and Moses)

Introduction to the
KINGDOM
of GOD

Jesus intrigued people. Some were impressed and attracted; others became irritated or felt threatened. Those who watched and listened carefully, ready to drop their presuppositions, realized He was inviting everyone to a new kind of life—kingdom life.

Jesus spent more time talking about the kingdom of God than almost any other subject. When we factor in His miracles, which demonstrated kingdom power, and His teaching about a different way of living, the kingdom was clearly His priority. Even His descriptions of God as Father hinge on the fact that God is a loving King in the business of expanding His kingdom—on earth as it is in heaven.

At the time, many people misunderstood Jesus, which prompts the question, do we? Typically, people today spend little time considering the meaning and implications of the kingdom of God for them. One reason is that the Bible is not laid out subject by subject like a reference tool; the Gospels derive from eyewitness accounts of everyday encounters and teaching sessions. Piecing together a coherent picture of any theme is hard. Add to that the fact that most of us focus on finding solutions for our pressing problems, and the kingdom of God remains some kind of mysterious theological theory.

However, Jesus' first ministry targets were precisely those pressing human problems. His miracles solved them; His teachings illuminated and untangled life. They showed His authority and wisdom, and gave Him credibility. People were blessed and praised God. But those of them (and us) who consider more deeply what Jesus did and said realize that, scattered among the Gospel accounts, they are just puzzle pieces inviting us to contemplate them more deeply. Then, for the picture to become clear, the pieces must be assembled. As the picture forms, we see ourselves in it, living the new life.

The sections of this book reflect the path that Jesus hoped people would follow once they accepted His invitation: understanding, entering, living, and spreading the kingdom. Most readers are already on that path, but many will find their bearings and get a confident spring in their steps forward by contemplating these short pieces. It will also help people to explain the kingdom to others.

These pieces are a collection of my own contemplations about Jesus' encounters. The process began a decade ago. It became focused during three years of reading the Gospels multiple times and studying other passages about the King and His kingdom. I analyzed Jesus' conversations and actions until patterns emerged. When, why, how, and to whom did He do miracles or deliver His parables? How many of these things had to do with the kingdom? What did Jesus' first followers finally understand their mission to be? The puzzling picture of the kingdom of God became clearer. It's a puzzle that no one person can assemble and it will never be complete in this life, but I pray this book will aid your reflections on Jesus' ministry and your participation in His kingdom.

UNDERSTANDING IT

FIGURING OUT JESUS

(Context: John 11:1–53.)

A dignified fluster, that's the best way to describe his entrance. The Pharisee flew through the chamber door where the high priest was meeting. He bowed awkwardly and stood there, robes slightly askew, panting, sweating, red-faced.

"Caiaphas, it's getting dangerous. People just came from Bethany saying that the Galilean's there and He's brought a dead man back to life after four days." The Pharisee snatched a breath. *"What are we doing? For this man is performing many signs. If we let Him go on like this, all men will believe in Him, and the Romans will come and take away both our place and our nation"* (John 11:47–48).

Put yourself in the place of an observer of Jesus over three years of His ministry until just before His Triumphal Entry. You might be a religious leader concerned to prevent heresy or rebellion. Perhaps you're an ordinary person wanting to be right with God and to know His presence. You have heard about His miracles and gleaned snippets of His teachings, but you know nothing of His birth, death, or resurrection. It would be like taking scissors to the Gospel accounts, snipping off both ends of each, and cutting out most of His teachings. Even the best-informed people knew no more, and most knew far less. At that point in history, everyone was trying to figure out Jesus from just those things.

Records give details of thirteen deliverances and about thirty healings. Jesus also made predictions that came true, walked on water, calmed storms, multiplied food, turned foot-wash into fine wine, produced taxes from fish and fish where there had been none, and raised three people from the dead.

The pattern in all these things is that there is almost no pattern. But notice: Jesus only did three healings at a distance; ninety percent happened when people met Jesus. Forty-five percent of healings included touch, and most happened with the simplest commands, comments, or actions. Two involved saliva! And, clearly, faith greased miracles—anyone's faith.

No method or formula stands out; the authoritative presence of Jesus is the common denominator. Jesus, seeing needs around Him, met them with power. He deliberately traveled through the region, often visiting new communities. Many of His works resulted in glory. At least forty percent of miracles and deliverances caused news about Him to spread: around Galilee and Judea, north to Phoenicia, and across the Jordan.

When we consider Jesus' message, the kingdom of God[1] was central to thirty out of ninety-six of His teachings; He usually mentioned it multiple times in each. That counts the Sermon on the Mount as one (it includes eight mentions). He often talked about it when explaining miracles and in arguments with religious leaders. In all, Jesus used the words "king" or "kingdom" when talking about the kingdom of God sixty-six times (lumping parallel Gospel accounts together as single events).

Later, Matthew summarized his observations this way: *Jesus was going about all the cities and the villages, teaching in their synagogues, and proclaiming the gospel of the kingdom, and healing every kind of disease and every kind of sickness.* (Matthew 9:35)

---

1. You have probably noticed that the phrase "kingdom of heaven" is used in some Scriptures. They mean the same thing.

Jesus stood out. He cared about needy people and used miraculous power to help them; it was easy for those people to rally behind Him. However, Jesus also triggered a flurry of questions about Himself and His message, especially from the religious leaders. "Could this really be the Messiah bringing the kingdom of God to earth according to prophecy and as He claims? On the other hand, He tends to mix with the wrong people and break Sabbath rules. According to the religious textbooks, those things don't go together. So, is He in league with the devil or anointed by God? In that case, heaven forbid, should we revise the textbooks?"

We probably don't have those exact questions, but it seems there is always a gap between human expectations about God and His ways, and their reality. Our expectations come from our cultures, languages, and even from our interpretations of Scripture. The gap influences our answers to our questions, and if it's wide, we might get flustered. The extent to which we cross the gap and relate to God as He really is depends on how far we pursue accurate answers.

What on earth is this Kingdom of God that Jesus proclaimed? It's essential for us to set aside our expectations and presuppositions and consider carefully what Jesus did and spoke.

DESCRIBING
a DIAMOND

(Context: Matthew 19:16–29. Parallels: Mark 10:17–27; Luke 18:18–27.)

One way to describe the indescribable is to use different words and analogies. It's like examining a diamond from different angles in varying lights. Several aspects of the spiritual life are like diamonds that we find difficult to comprehend and explain. Even the Bible finds them hard to describe. The Bible and Bible teachers sometimes sound confusing because they use different terms. For example, what exactly is the reward of our faith, the result of our decision to accept Jesus as Lord? Is it salvation, or eternal life, or heaven, or a place in His kingdom? Frustratingly, the answer is "Yes."

One good source that helps untangle the confusion is the parable of the rich, young ruler. In Matthew's account, the man asks Jesus how to obtain eternal life. Jesus tells him to sell his possessions, give the proceeds to the poor, and gain treasure in heaven. When the man backs away from that challenge, Jesus says, "*It is hard for a rich man to enter the kingdom of heaven,*" harder than getting a camel through the eye of a needle. (Whatever that means, it sounds pretty hard!) Finally, the disciples ask, "Then who can be saved?" Mark and Luke agree with Matthew. All three writers connect four things:[2]

---

2. John 3:3–5, 15–16 seem to link the kingdom, eternal life, and salvation. Other passages connect two of the four. Kingdom and eternal life (Matt. 25:34,46; Mark 9:43, 45, 47),

Eternal life.

Treasure in heaven.

Entry to the kingdom of heaven/God.

Being "saved."

Isolate any of those ideas and reflect on it long enough, and it becomes dull, and its relevance fades. People say they don't want to live forever because worshipping God on a cloud with a harp sounds boring. "Being saved" begs the question, what are we saved from? And it has its own set of confusing language: We "surrender our lives to Him," "get born again," or "become believers." In the absence of slick advertising, "heavenly treasure" has little attraction. And the idea of the kingdom of God is as barren as a desert—except for the King. It's in Him that we see the diamond sparkle.

The four ideas all connect to God, the King. Jesus defined eternal life as knowing the Father and Himself (John 17:3). Heaven is the dwelling of God. You won't find it using mapping apps—He's Spirit. We are privileged to dwell with Him (John 14:1–3). Salvation is not only *from* sin and its consequences; it's *into* adoption as the King's children and into His abundant lifestyle (John 10:10). Entering His kingdom begins with subjecting ourselves to His rule, but continues as He teaches us to join with Him, extend His kingdom, and reign with Him. All four are about our relationship with Him.

The rich ruler walked away from the diamond. Jesus makes us the same offer. If you think that following Jesus means living a life that is different but somewhat parallel to non-followers, you are mistaken. Jesus goes another, sometimes opposite, way. We swim against the current of "normal" life on earth by, for instance, giving away what we treasure here or surrendering our control and goals. To live His life, we must be born again

---

eternal life and salvation (John 5:24, 29, 34, 39; 10:9–10, 28). Elsewhere, other things are connected. For example, perfection and the regeneration or rebirth at the reign of the Son of Man (Matt. 19:21, 28).

to a spirit life (John 3:3–5). Flesh and blood cannot inherit the kingdom of God, only spiritual beings can (1 Cor. 15:50). God is spirit; we relate to Him in spirit.

Life in the King's family is like an indescribably beautiful diamond. The four items mentioned in the story are the same diamond seen from different angles.

HEADLINE NEWS

(Context: Mark 1:14–15. Parallel: Matthew 4:12–17.)

Most people who have followed Jesus for a year or two understand that a simple belief in the existence of God is not enough. They know a way to counter that trite idea: "Even demons believe, but they tremble" (James 2:19). Genuine followers believe many things about God and His ways; Jesus' first message contains the core of our beliefs:

> *The time is fulfilled,*
> *And the kingdom of God is at hand;*
> *Repent and believe in the gospel.* (Mark 1:15)

"Gospel" is not an everyday word. It's used almost exclusively in church circles; it's "Christianese." Uncommon words quickly become mysterious and meaningless to many people. In everyday language, Jesus called people to believe in the "good news." And that, of course, raises questions: good news about what? And why is belief in a news report so important? Shouldn't we simply believe in Jesus?

Isaiah presented an early newsflash in beautiful poetry: "How lovely on the mountains are the feet of him who brings good news" (Isa. 52:7). The news was about the restoration of Jerusalem after her enemies had invaded and trashed her. The messenger's cry was simple: "Your God reigns." Earlier,

Jerusalem herself had been told to deliver related news, "Here is your God" (Isa. 40:9–10).

The news hangs on those three words: "Your God reigns." It explodes with implications. Reigning is what kings do. If God is good, is King over all kings, and if He uses His power to care for His people, then news of His reign is tremendous. Breaking stories will never bump it from the headlines. The people of Jerusalem could rejoice. God knew their oppression, shame, poverty, and suffering. He was about to intervene sovereignly to save them from their troubles. Comfort, joy, and complete wellbeing were coming.

When Jesus announced that the time was fulfilled, He was talking about Himself. The King, His Father, had sent Him to bring the kingdom to earth. Part of the news that Jesus called everyone to believe in was His own arrival. For three years, He demonstrated and explained life in the kingdom. Astute observers would surely see how good that life could be. Then, in His death and resurrection, He blew away every obstacle to a royal relationship.

In a sense, there are three parts to the good news that we believe:

- The arrival of the King's Son, the Messiah. The kingdom was finally "at hand."
- The goodness of the King and His kingdom.
- The invitation to everyone to become a child and subject of the King.

God and His work are inseparable because what He does flows from who He is. Believing in the good news begins with believing in Him.

STRETCH EXERCISES

(Context: Luke 7:17–35. Parallel: Matthew 11:2–19.)

Good athletes prepare themselves for events with various warm-ups, including stretch exercises. Stretching helps avoid injuries to the muscles, tendons, and ligaments. It also prepares the body to go to the next level of performance. A series of interactions in Luke seems to address a similar spiritual need—preparing for the kingdom of God.

The passage begins with a question from John the Baptist. "Are you the Expected One?" Jesus listed a short resumé of His work, using a prophetic job description of the Messiah as a comparison. But one item could not be checked off the list—prisoners (like John) had to wait for freedom and vengeance. Jesus was the Expected One, but not in the expected way. That was a stretch for John. Would he accept the messianic evidence or stumble over the missing piece because his gnawing need was not being met? Jesus concluded His answer with the following comment:

> *"I say to you, among those born of women, there is no one greater than John, yet he who is least in the kingdom of God is greater than he." When all the people and the tax collectors heard this, they acknowledged God's justice, having been baptized with the baptism of John. But the Pharisees and the lawyers rejected God's purpose for themselves, not having been baptized by John.* (Luke 7:28–30)

Jesus affirmed John as a great prophet. But then He stretched the crowd's minds too. Every subject of the kingdom of God surpassed this great man. So, kingdom membership must be extremely valuable. The least in the kingdom is greater because kingdom life begins with Spirit birth as well as water baptism. The idea produced two reactions.

Notice how we humans behave. When it comes to new ideas, we tend to accept things that build on our existing views and lifestyles. We prefer affirmation and reinforcement; we often reject arguments that challenge us or require us to backpedal. Those who had accepted John's baptism said, "That's right," to the idea.[3] The religious leaders, who rejected John, gave no place[4] to the counsel or purpose of God for themselves.

Now there's a challenge for us! If we are to find the purpose of God for our lives, we must be prepared to humbly discard old worldviews and practices whenever they are contrary to God's ways. Receiving John's baptism was the sign of a soft heart—a readiness to repent. Thoughts and actions had to change because the kingdom had arrived (Matt. 3:2). For those who accepted, John's baptism functioned like a warm-up exercise for the kingdom. Hard hearts were unable to repent, receive baptism, or embrace the kingdom. And today, fans, foes, and fallen people all need to "repent" in some way to make room for the kingdom.

Jesus went on to describe the spiritual climate in terms of children playing Weddings and Funerals. Other awkward children refused to join in with either game. Many responses to John and Jesus had been like that; they frowned on John's stoic life and on Jesus' celebration of freedom. Jesus concluded that "wisdom is vindicated[5] by all her children." It's a blunt hint and a huge stretch for religious[6] minds, but ordinary people and tax-gatherers

---

3. *Edikaiosan* means justifying God, making Him righteous, or vindicating Him. But those translations would make no sense.
4. "Gave no place" is closer to the Greek meaning.
5. *Edikaiothe* is another form of the word meaning justify or made righteous.
6. Throughout this book, I use words like "religion" for either the Jewish religion of Jesus' day or for a system of Christian beliefs and practices that seems to agree with biblical

were God's children. They had accepted baptism and the idea that kingdom membership was important (v. 29). They had no problem associating with a friend of sinners—they were sinners!

When God seems to be doing something in your circumstances—something uncomfortable but not unbiblical—perhaps the best advice is, "stretch … and hold."

---

theology but lacks the power of a living relationship with God modeled by Jesus with His Father. However, I am not the judge of who the label fits in the second case or of the outcome of that kind of religion.

NOT *for* HIRE

(Context: John 6:1–15, 22–58.)

Jesus probably felt like a square peg stuffed into a round hole one spring day in Galilee. He had just fed five thousand people, who turned out to be hungry for more than bread and fish. They longed for a Messiah and expected him to be another prophet like Moses, as Moses had predicted (Deut. 18:15). Moses had an impressive track record for answering prayers when it came to food and water. When Jesus multiplied a boy's lunch, the crowd jumped to the conclusion that Jesus was that prophesied Messiah (John 6:14).

The Messiah was not limited to the role of prophet. The crowning role was that of king. In fact, most threads of messianic expectation involved a king. The messianic king would lead Israel into glory days like those she had enjoyed under King David. "Down with corrupt religious leaders! Down with the Roman occupiers! Down with taxes!" yelled the crowds. Israel had been without a real king for five hundred years; it was time to fill the vacancy. Other candidates had caught the attention of recruiters in recent years, but they had failed to deliver. A miraculous free meal for five thousand was a promising sign. The crowd was ready to crown Jesus king. However, Jesus surprised them—He slipped away (John 6:15).

Ever perceptive, Jesus saw two huge problems with the flattering job offer. Next day, after the crowd had tracked Jesus down, He tried to correct their misconceptions:

Jesus answered them and said, "Truly, truly, I say to you, you seek Me, not because you saw signs, but because you ate of the loaves and were filled. Do not work for the food which perishes, but for the food which endures to eternal life, which the Son of Man will give to you, for on Him the Father, God, has set His seal." Therefore they said to Him, "What shall we do, so that we may work the works of God?" Jesus answered and said to them, "This is the work of God, that you believe in Him whom He has sent." (John 6:26–29)

The crowd had rallied behind Jesus because He provided for their practical needs. It was one of several wrong motives. They selected Him as a promising candidate to be king because they hoped for more meals, miracles, and an uprising to oust the Romans. Jesus cares about people and gladly performs miracles, but not military coups. He wants us to pursue a higher priority—food with an eternal shelf-life.

The conversation that follows is one of the most complex that Jesus had. First, Jesus clarified that Moses was not the manna-maker; the Father had provided it. Similarly, the Father had sent Jesus as living bread that must be "eaten"—absorbed into one's life. That "absorption" happens when we believe Jesus is the Son of God with all that implies. Belief (or faith) means accepting His claims and then responding to those claims wholeheartedly.

You see, the crowd also had a wrong idea about kingship. Kings are not elected to do the will of the people; real kings make the rules. They don't respond to "Wanted" advertisements. Our obedience is His coronation. Jesus alluded to taking the bread and wine of the Lord's Supper because that act requires faith and obedience. We take it because of faith in His sacrifice on the cross and in resurrection life—His and ours. He commanded us to partake, and we obey, along with all the other things He calls us to—because He is King.

What about you? Are you only interested in what Jesus can do for you? Do you have a set of expectations that He must fulfill to satisfy you? Or are you getting to know the real King Jesus, listening to His claims, and responding to His commands?

The
BOOK ENDS

(Context: Matthew 13:24–30, 36–43, 47–50.)

The kingdom of heaven may be compared to a man who sowed good seed in his field. But while men were sleeping, his enemy came and sowed tares also among the wheat, and went away. (Matthew 13:24–25)

What kind of king would allow an enemy to contaminate his wheat? Most kings would construct a fence and set a guard if necessary. Only the weakest would even allow an enemy to remain resourceful enough to contaminate his fields. Not much of a king, eh? Perhaps the disciples were thinking something like that when they asked Jesus to explain the parable of the wheat and the tares. Jesus' explanation did a few things: it identified Him as the farmer, accepted an active devil, and stretched the kingdom timeline to the conclusion of history. It also linked it to the Parable of the Dragnet, making those two parables bookends that prop up four other kingdom parables on the shelf of Matthew thirteen.

So much for stories. Two thousand years of experiencing a world of rampant evil have produced a harvest of cynicism. What kind of kingdom doesn't consolidate its rule immediately? How many people reject Jesus because of the untreated disease of suffering? How many believers are weakened by waiting? Who hasn't been tempted to take a hoe or flamethrower to those tares or to do what amounts to self-isolating in sanitized greenhouses, feeding on only positive kingdom news? It takes faith to live in God's weedy field.

It takes a certain kind of ears too—ears that are tuned to the kingdom message. Ears like that are not distracted or clogged; they hear, and the message reaches the heart.[7] The message is two-pronged: the kingdom is coming and it's good, but it's not yet here in full. In the waiting period, evil persists. The bookends face us with mixture and a seemingly looong wait. The other four parables in the set boost faith because they tell us that, while the kingdom starts tiny, it expands and is so precious that savvy investors exchange everything for it.

The last book of the Bible also builds faith. Whether or not it tells of the end of history (scholars disagree), it describes the intensity of the struggle between Satan and our King. Jesus is always victorious even though His people may suffer. In the final harvest at the end of the age, the tares will be removed and the catch sorted.

I glimpsed the sorting once. While walking along an African beach, I met some locals. Two of them were rowing a dugout canoe into the sea, towing a dragnet behind them, while the rest held one end on the shore. When the canoe returned with the other end of the net, the group allowed me to help them pull on the two ends and drag the net in like a giant sack. When we got it to the beach, it was full of various things: sticks, jellyfish, a crab, seaweed, unidentified trash, a young shark, a stingray, and a few nice fish. No problem, toss back the rubbish and keep the decent fish.

Satan and his evil agents will, in the end, be destroyed. Those who have resisted his temptation to despair, compromise, lawlessness, and unbelief, and have remained faithful will stand before the King to receive their reward.

---

7. This is the point of Jesus' Parable about Parables in Matthew 13:1–23.

MAKING ISRAEL GREAT AGAIN

(Context: Acts 1:1–8.)

Straddling two positions is awkward—spiritually too. Jesus' followers live in two kingdoms—the kingdom of God and that of the world. The world is inescapably close and screams; God's kingdom comes slow and gentle, like sprouting corn. Its fullness lies in a misty future. It's easy to become confused.

Six weeks after Jesus rose from the dead, His disciples still put their weight on the wrong foot. They asked:

> *"Lord, is it at this time that You are restoring the kingdom to Israel?" But He said to them, "It is not for you to know periods of time or appointed times which the Father has set by His own authority; but you will receive power when the Holy Spirit has come upon you; and you will be My witnesses."* (Acts 1:6–8)

Their question reveals what excited them and how limited their understanding of God's plan still was. The resurrection had proved that Jesus was Lord and Messiah (Acts 2:36; Rom. 1:4). But, like other Jews, they expected the Messiah to make Israel great again. "Out with the Romans." "Down with corrupt leaders and traitorous tax-gatherers. (Not you, Matthew. You're Okay.)" "Jesus is King." As loyal Jewish disciples, those were their heart cries.

26

Eventually, Jesus disses everyone's illusions and bursts everyone's bubbles. Not this time. Jesus hardly acknowledged their question. No correction. No explanation. No need! Things were moving right along: Ascension, Pentecost ten days later, and then a divinely orchestrated outpouring of the Spirit on (cough) a Roman stronghold. That outpouring finally opened Peter's eyes to God's plan for a pan-ethnic kingdom extending beyond tiny Israel's borders.

Whatever excites us and fills our expectations becomes a source of anxiety when it is threatened. That's why Peter had grabbed a sword to protect his king (John 18:10). And it's why we get riled about so much on earth: politics, economics, climate change, bad laws, and broken laws. You've read the petitions and placards. As citizens of two kingdoms, only clarity about the kingdom of God will free us from anxiety and swordplay. Jesus was clear. In one of His rare answers to Pilate, He assured the governor that His kingdom was not of this world and did not require a fight (John 18:36).

As with all the seed-like words of Jesus, this truth about the kingdom will fall on various heart surfaces. Some will be hard, some distracted, but others will take encouragement and grow more fruitful as Jesus' witnesses. So, let's prepare our hearts. Then, to paraphrase one of Jesus' favorite endings, if we have spiritual ears, let's use them (Matt. 13:9).

WHEN *and* WHERE

(Context: Luke 17:20–37. Parallels: Matthew 24:23–44; Mark 13:32–37.)

I'm pretty sure I once walked into Uganda. I was in Kenya, hiking with friends up fourteen-thousand-foot Mount Elgon, an extinct volcano. The unmarked border passes through the crater and I hiked around the rim. Like that border, the kingdom of God seems frustratingly indistinct to some people. We like to know details—things like when and where. The Pharisees traced religious borders to know where everyone stood (convinced, of course, that they were inside). So, they asked Jesus (probably cynically) when His kingdom was coming. He replied:

> *The kingdom of God is not coming with signs to be observed* [careful observation]; *nor will they say, "Look, here it is!" Or, "There it is!" For behold, the kingdom of God is in your midst.* (Luke 17:20–21)

Jesus said His kingdom is not observable or locatable, perhaps because it is rooted in hearts. It does not conform to tidy religious expectations. Most of all, it had already begun, though it was (and is) incomplete. Ironically, the religious leaders were missing the kingdom. It was staring them in their faces because the King and His subjects were in their midst.

Kingdom is inseparable from the King. In a sense, the kingdom and the presence of Jesus, the King, are equivalent. Jesus said something similar about His presence: "Where two or three have gathered together in My name, there I am *in their midst*."[8] The phrase "in My name" connects Jesus' presence in a gathering with His kingdom. To act in God's name means to act according to His will and ways. It implies being subject to His rule, extending it, and seeking His righteousness. Jesus' subjects act with His authority and experience His provision and empowerment as they do. The King, and now His followers, induce kingdom around them as a magnet induces a field in nearby iron objects. But the kingdom awaits completion.

(Luke 17:22–24) The Jews understood that history would end with a day of the Lord's judgment and the full arrival of His kingdom. In the rest of the chapter, Jesus addressed that misty idea. He warned His disciples not to chase after rumors of localized concentrations of the presence of God. The Son of Man will blaze everywhere, suddenly, like lightning.

(Luke 17:26–36) Amazingly, not everyone will drop everything for Him. Jesus knew human nature and history. Ordinary life (eating, drinking, marrying, buying, selling, planting, building) is all fine and good, but every society has sin mixed in. Rather than ignore sin, or live oblivious of it, Jesus' subjects must do ordinary life differently, injecting righteousness, and being kingdom inducers. At the same time, they must be alert, so that, when the Son of Man arrives, they drop their ordinary lives, exchanging them for the fuller kingdom. But humans don't focus well or remain alert for long. Like Noah and Lot's neighbors, most people scoff and continue life as usual.

Learning to exchange lifestyles is part of following Jesus. Jesus encountered people who thought they wanted to follow Him but were unwilling to make the exchange (Luke 9:57–62; 18:18–27). For them, possessions or relationships were too valuable. Possessions and money appear to give us leverage over life, indicate successful accumulation, and assure us of security. But they rob us of dependency on God. It's easy to claim that God provides, but until we establish a flow of generous giving, we do not really experience the kingdom lifestyle of receiving from the Father to serve Him and pass some on to the needy. Without that experience, we tend to resort to our clingy old

---

8. Matt. 18:20. See too Matt. 28:20.

ways next time. When we hold loosely to what many call "life," we find true life. When we build protective walls around "life," we miss out on real life (Luke 17:33).

Ever inquisitive, the disciples wanted to know "where?" (Luke 17:37). They seem to have missed the point. Given the predicted, pitiful response to His second coming, Jesus' cryptic answer probably means "everywhere." Lightning and soaring scavengers are visible for miles. Death attracts lovers of death; scavengers catch the stench of easily-picked carcasses. In Jesus' examples, only fifty percent of people chose kingdom life over its handier, terminally sick substitute. In the end, there will be spiritual casualties.

There's a simple response to the vagueness about the kingdom: draw close to the King and learn His ways. The closer we are to Him, the more we will experience His kingdom.

ENTERING IT

Jump Aboard

(Context: Luke 10:1–24. See also Matthew 10:5–42.)

"Tuende! Tuende!" Shouted the ferry captain. "Let's go!" Boarding the ferry to the island of Lamu on the coast of Kenya, with a forty-pound backpack, was tricky. It was important to start well-balanced, time the jump with the rising surge of the boat, and land as squarely as possible, hoping someone would grab and steady me. There was no time to wait; the ferry was full, belching diesel fumes, revving to leave.

Entering the kingdom of God is rather like that leap. John the Baptist and Jesus both shouted the equivalent of "Tuende!" "The kingdom of God is at hand" (Matt. 3:2; 4:17; Mark 1:15). The phrase suggests the kingdom is hovering in the circumstances and encounters of life, waiting to be plucked. There is some truth in that idea. However, every time the phrase appears, it is in the perfect aspect (complete but with ongoing implications) and means "the kingdom of God has come near." The boat has docked. It's time to jump on board.

Entering the kingdom requires us to leave one stable place and move to another through an awkward transition. Life without Jesus seems stable; a blend of illusions of control and reliability. Leaping a gap to the unknown is uncomfortable, even when we are assured the landing place is safe and pleasant, as in Jesus' words, "Repent and believe the *good news*" (Mark 1:15).

That message wasn't just John and Jesus' responsibility; proclaiming the kingdom is the task for everyone who follows Jesus.

> *Whatever city you enter, and they receive you, eat what is set before you; and heal those in it who are sick, and say to them, "The kingdom of God has come near to you." But whatever city you enter and they do not receive you, go out into its streets and say, "Even the dust of your city which clings to our feet, we wipe off in protest against you; yet be sure of this, that the kingdom of God has come near."* (Luke 10:8–11. See also Luke 9:60.)

- It's a message for towns and villages, markets and streets, homes (and boats), not just religious places and special meetings. Sometimes people come; mostly, messengers go to where people are.
- It's a message accompanied by demonstrations. Jesus healed sick people as a sign of the reality, goodness, and power of the King who rules the kingdom.
- It's a message for receptive "people of peace" and an indictment of the unreceptive. The kingdom is real, whether it's accepted or not.

The message begs the question: If this kingdom is so caring, real, and powerful, what's it all about? There's really only one way to find out—by jumping on board and lending a hand to others to do the same.

HEAVEN'S SALES STRATEGY

(Context: Luke 10:1–16. Parallel: Matthew 11:20–24.)

Tours of Israel never include Sodom and Gomorrah; they were wiped off the map so thoroughly that we hardly know where to look for ashes. Tyre and Sidon survived, but they're in Lebanon. Many tourists to Galilee visit Capernaum, where Jesus lived for a while; Bethsaida and Chorazin get a few. Sadly, all three are in ruins—archaeologically interesting but uninhabited. It happened just as Jesus warned that it would. Here's a clip:

> *Whatever city you enter and they do not receive you, go out into its streets and say, "Even the dust of your city which clings to our feet, we wipe off in protest against you; yet be sure of this, that the kingdom of God has come near." I say to you, it will be more tolerable in that day for Sodom, than for that city. Woe to you Chorazin! Woe to you Bethsaida! For if the miracles had been performed in Tyre and Sidon which occurred in you, they would have repented long ago, sitting in sackcloth and ashes.* (Luke 10:10–13)

The cities that Jesus and His disciples often hung out in had buzzed with news of this superstar's miracles, but nothing changed. If the ancient, disreputable cities of Tyre and Sidon had witnessed such wonders, they would have repented. Instead, once the puzzled excitement wore off, Galilean life

35

returned to normal, proving that they had harder hearts than the ancients. The miracles were evidence of heaven's kingdom reordering fallen earth.[9] The logical response was to welcome and host the messengers, find out more, and rearrange one's life to experience more of that beautiful kingdom.

How do we respond to spiritual superstars? Do we chase after everyone who displays miraculous powers? Do we rush from event to event to see the next big shower of signs? Are we so focused on their charisma or lavish give-aways that we miss the point God is making through them?

Superstars and signs are frequently legitimate. They certainly were in those Galilean towns. But what is the point? Are they only to bless those who are healed and delivered, or do they have another purpose? Jesus was clearly disappointed, saddened, and perhaps angry that His miracles did not change Galilean society. The blessing on needy people and the glory that goes to God still stand. But when the King signals His benevolent presence, surely it's time to get on His side. In a sense, miracles are heaven's sales strategy. Give people a taste and some will buy in for more.

Miracles prompt us to turn from our old ways and adopt His. Turning is the essential step for entering the kingdom of God.

---

9. Luke 11:20 is another example.

ROAD WORK

(Context: Luke 3:1–18. Parallels: Matthew 3:1–12; Mark 1:2–8; John 1:19–31.)

Would you invite John the Baptist to a social gathering? Perhaps not. He was eccentric and blunt. When Luke says that John preached *good* news (gospel), it comes as quite a surprise to those who know his style.

> *He came into all the district around the Jordan, preaching a baptism of repentance for the forgiveness of sins … With many other exhortations also he preached the gospel to the people.* (Luke 3:3, 18)

At first glance, repentance and exhortations do not sound like good news. Is it any wonder that people cross the street to avoid megaphone messages that basically say, "Repent sinner"? Repentance is associated with an admission of guilt, which easily induces shame. So, what is the connection between good news and repentance?

We find the answer in the context of the passage. Earlier, Luke quotes Isaiah 40:3–5, which talks about the crooked (*skolios*) becoming straight. *Skolios* is the word from which we name "scoliosis," a spine-twisting condition in which something is painfully out of line.[10] John understood his role

---

10. In Acts 2:40, Peter mentioned the perverse (*skolios*) generation when he shared good news with the crowd.

as a bulldozer for the King, making His path straight.[11] For crooked things to become straight, there has to be a change. If we were to talk to people about changed thinking and changed behavior that will straighten out the kinks in their lives, they might be more receptive.

Changed behavior explains why John the Baptist was so insistent on seeing fruit from repentance. When people started asking, "What shall we do?" it was the first sign of genuine repentance (Luke 3:10, 12, 14; Acts 2:37). John had a ready answer because he understood the practical ways of the King: share what you have with those who have less; don't be greedy but be content; be honest; stop exploiting people; be gentle; speak the truth.

Some of Jesus' first words were exactly the same as John's. "Repent for the kingdom of heaven is at hand" (Matt. 3:2; 4:17). The good news is about a wonderful King who restores us to His family. But the way into His kingdom is a freshly-graded road—a hearty pursuit of godly behavior. Imagine getting a clean, new road straight to the royal palace. That's what repentance does. I think you'll agree, it is good news after all.

---

11. See: John Avery, *The Name Quest—Explore the Names of God to Grow in Faith and Get to Know Him Better*, (Morgan James Publishing, 2015), 260–262.

CHANGING SPIRITUAL CITIZENSHIP

(Context: Matthew 3:1–12; 4:12–17. Parallel: Mark 1:14–15.)

"Repent, for the kingdom of heaven is at hand." (Matthew 3:2; 4:17)

We tend to think of repentance in terms of sin (and perhaps its siblings, transgression and iniquity). However, when John the Baptist and Jesus called for repentance, they were speaking of a change of citizenship. Leave the kingdom of the world and exchange life there for life in the kingdom of God. Turning from sin is just part of it.

In 2018, my wife and I became citizens of the USA through a process known as naturalization. Paul didn't know that word, but spiritual naturalization is what Jesus accomplished for us on the cross. "He delivered us from the domain of darkness, and transferred us to the kingdom of His beloved Son, in whom we have redemption, the forgiveness of sins" (Col. 1:13–14). It sounds complete. Legally it is, but like many aspects of kingdom life, there are two phases. What is true legally still has to be worked out in our lives and our world. The kingdom has arrived but not yet fully. That is why Paul's statement follows his prayer for increased knowledge of God and a life worthy of Him.

Like Israel, immediately after Jericho's walls had crumbled, we stand on the border of a promised land. God has decreed that it is ours, but we must conquer it and learn to live in it. Repentance is part of that process. Don't think of repentance as a step of brokenness, taken in tears, doubled up on the carpet at the front of a church. That's fine. Of course it is right to repent when we are convicted of particular sins, but repentance is more. It is the humble admission that we are entering a better land and need to shed the old life for the new so we can thoroughly experience the new.

The word "repent" implies a change of thinking that leads to a change of behavior. No earthly society or culture functions entirely in the way God's kingdom does, including the most Christian ones. No matter what our thinking is rooted in, it is usually different from God's thinking (Isa. 55:8–9). Some aspects of our cultures do not clash with His; God redeems many parts to His glory. But we must hold to our roots loosely while we embrace God's thoughts in order to share His ways.

Even the least sinful of us has a lifetime of opportunity to make the exchange. The norms of human existence color every tiny decision, action, and word. It varies depending on our family, community, culture, etc., but those norms are essentially foreign to the kingdom of God. My present way of thinking and living must bow to a new way of thinking and living. Repenting for the kingdom requires a lifestyle surrendered to the probing of the Holy Spirit. He will teach us how to leave the old way and naturalize us to the new way—the kingdom life.

DRIVING
on the RIGHT SIDE

(Context: Matthew 3:1–6; 4:12–17. Parallel: Mark 1:14–15.)

Being bi-cultural is difficult. I refer to people who live successfully in different cultures at different times. Perhaps they are missionaries, refugees, expatriate workers, or part of a marriage that bridges two cultures. I experience it to a degree when I go from the USA to the United Kingdom, where I grew up. After a few hours of extra concentration, I adjust to driving on a different side of the street. My English accent is not always understood by Americans and is so Americanized that English people comment on it. In many ways, I think and act like an American; yet I immediately understand what British people are thinking and why. I can fit well in both cultures, though not one hundred percent in either. I'm more informal than most British people but more reserved than many Americans.

Christians usually don't realize it, but every one of us is bi-cultural. We're getting used to heaven, but the motherland clings to us. We need frequent reminders of the first rallying cry of John the Baptist and Jesus. It was like the flight attendant's announcement when a plane touches down in a foreign country. "Welcome to the kingdom of heaven. Please remember to drive on the right side of the road!"

Now in those days John the Baptist came, preaching in the wilderness of Judea, saying, "Repent, for the kingdom of heaven is at hand."
(Matthew 3:1–2. See also 4:17.)

Notice the context of the two announcements. John preached in Judea, the Jewish heartland. The ordinary people seemed to respond well, but when the religious leaders slithered up, John challenged them, "Bring forth fruit in keeping with repentance" (Matt. 3:7–12). John had come to dynamite religious obstacles that blocked the path to a relationship with God. His call for repentance was about as welcome as explosives in a museum.

Jesus waited until the authorities had imprisoned John. Then He began work in Galilee where the locals had a reputation for non-conformity to religious and political niceties. Many Galileans were labeled as sinners. Exactly the same announcement on Jesus' lips conveyed a message of freedom. To humble Galileans who paid attention, repentance spelled release from bondage and light dispelling darkness.

The kingdom culture is different from any culture on earth. Even exemplary Christians must humbly accept that God's ways are higher than our brightest and best ways. The word "repent" includes the idea of changed thinking, but it implies changed behavior too. Any thoughts and actions that are contrary to life in the kingdom of heaven are sinful and need to change.

I find myself struggling with my two spiritual cultures in two ways. Sometimes I try to live the Christian life in a worldly way, applying the world's resources and values to good ends. For instance, I depend on harder work or a bigger investment of money in Christian projects, rather than seeking God for fruit in those projects. A more subtle struggle is when I live the worldly life in a Christian way, applying Christian behavior and seeking God's provision and protection for my own subtly hidden goals—and my own glory, not His.

Of course, we all shuttle from the kingdom of darkness to the kingdom of heaven the moment we repent and believe in Jesus. Yet in this life, we will always be bi-cultural and feel a tug from the world. We have a lifetime to adapt to the culture of the kingdom, to "get with the flow" of kingdom "traffic." Let's start by making it a habit to ask what the objectives of the King are and what the methods of the kingdom are. The kingdom life can only be fully lived in the power of the Spirit, seeing life through God's eyes, and depending on His help to accomplish His will for His kingdom.

The PARABLE *about* PARABLES

(Context: Matthew 13:1–23. Parallels: Mark 4:1–20; Luke 8:4–15.)

Story time was over. The keel of the fishing boat ground into the gravel along the shore, and the men stopped rowing. Jesus climbed over the side and paddled to the beach. As He and the disciples gathered their gear and prepared to go back to the house to rest, one of the disciples raised the question they had all been too shy to ask until the crowd dispersed.

"Why do you speak to them in parables?"

I think we get stuck in the Parable of the Soils.[12] What I mean is that we spend so much time trying to decipher the analogies and apply them to our lives that we miss the core of what Jesus said. This is one of Jesus' most important teachings because it answers the disciples' question, "Why do you speak to them in parables?" Jesus' answer is the key to hearing the voice of God and, therefore, the key to spiritual growth.

So, why did Jesus use parables? At first, His explanation seems cryptic:

---

12. Calling it the Parable of the Sower doesn't help.

Jesus answered them, "To you it has been granted to know the myster-
ies of the kingdom of heaven, but to them it has not been granted …
Therefore I speak to them in parables; because while seeing they do not
see, and while hearing they do not hear, nor do they understand …
But blessed are your eyes, because they see; and your ears, because
they hear. (Matthew 13:11, 13, 16)

Every crowd listening to Jesus' teaching contains two types of people; those who have functioning spiritual ears and eyes, and those who do not. Ears receptive to sound waves and eyes able to resolve light patterns are not enough. Spiritual sight and hearing happen when the heart understands, the mind perceives, and lives return to a healthy relationship with God (Matt. 13:14–15). The disciples were spiritually receptive; they could grasp the mysteries of the kingdom of God and change to live the kingdom lifestyle. You see, Jesus used parables to discover which people were in which group. The Parable of the Soils illustrates this essential lesson.

Every parable and truth about the King and His kingdom acts in the same way. Like a seed, it tests the soil of the heart. Many people hear God speaking directly to them, or through His followers, but only superficially. The truth is quickly snatched away from hard hearts. Difficult times, when temptation or opposition come, shrivel it. Distractions steal all time and energy, hindering application. Only hearts that are like soft, deep, and clean soil will apply the truth in such a way that life changes. Every time that Jesus concludes with the phrase, "He who has ears to hear, let him hear," He means the ears of the will.

So, next time God drops a seed of truth into your life, will your will nurture it to fruition?

CHILDLIKENESS

(Context: Matthew 18:1–10; John 3:1–21.)

Life in the kingdom of God is easy, but living it to the full is hard. It's easy because our part is basically passive—trusting and depending on God. It's hard because living that way is so contrary to human nature—adult human nature.

To the disciples, Jesus said, *"Unless you are converted [changed/turned] and become like children, you shall not enter the kingdom of heaven. Whoever then humbles himself as this child, he is the greatest in the kingdom of heaven."* (Matthew 18:3–4[13])

Jesus puzzled Nicodemus when He said, *"Unless one is born of water and the Spirit, he cannot enter into the kingdom of God."* He went on to explain that someone born of the Spirit looks like a leaf blowing in the wind. Understandably, Nicodemus asked, "How can these things be?" (John 3:5, 9). Quite so. We spend years being told to "grow up," and Jesus seems to say, "grow down."

Adults like to think they appear independent, competent, promising, or accomplished. Young children care little for those things. Spiritual rebirth into childlikeness requires humility and a radical shift in thinking. However, not everything about children is good. So, how can we be childlike without

---

13. See also Matt. 19:14; Mark 10:14–15; Luke 18:15–17.

being childish? Jesus focused on humility because it encompasses many aspects of childlikeness in a healthy family:

- Children adore their parents; they have no reason to substitute idols for them. They depend on their parents. They trust them for their safety and provision. Kids don't manage their own schedules. They listen and obey out of love and trust.
- Children don't care much what they do; being with parents is everything. When we learn that, we can let go of our need to establish and maintain a stable life with its demanding goals and routines. We can live an adventure with the Father, always listening and prepared for the next opportunity, because we are holding His hand.
- Children receive gifts gladly. They giggle, unwrap them, investigate, and run off to play with them. They're bold to ask for things too. However, human fathers have limited time and energy. They can only be in one place. Inevitably, children do not always get a perfect response, so they learn to manipulate, beg, and demand. They notice that fathers sometimes manipulate them and condition their love on performance, so they learn to strive. But in healthy father-child relationships, children know that they can go to their father and get the answer that is best for their health, happiness, and maturity. If his response differs from their original request, he will explain why later. That's how our heavenly Father is.
- Children know they are children; they accept their need to learn and grow. They know their parents are preparing them to face new situations. Mistakes and wrong reactions along the way are just opportunities to adjust behavior or be better prepared next time.
- Children show their feelings. As N. T. Wright pointed out, tears are not childish; they're childlike.[14] Children often want to turn compassion into action when they see others in pain and need. They have little concern about limited resources when they have experienced reliable provision.

---

14. N. T. Wright, *Following Jesus*, (Wm. B. Eerdmans Publishing Co., 1994), 58.

Maturity does not mean leaving childlike dependency; it means becoming a healthily dependent child of God. Spiritual children look to the Father for provision, protection, and answers to their questions. They see no need for alternative sources. Approaching the Father teachable and excited is natural. To enter the kingdom of God as a child is the same as entering the presence of the best of fathers—the King.

The
GAP

(Context: Mark 12:28–34. Parallel: Matthew 22:34–40.)

Not all Pharisees were bad; occasionally one would respond positively to Jesus.[15] An unnamed scribe (the scribes were a sub-group of the Pharisees) even said he wanted to follow Jesus (Matt. 8:19). After an argument between Jesus and some Sadducees, another scribe asked Jesus what the greatest commandment was. Jesus quoted the Law about loving God and others, and the scribe agreed with His answer. Then Jesus made a thought-provoking comment.

> *When Jesus saw that [the scribe] had answered intelligently, He said to him, "You are not far from the kingdom of God." (Mark 12:34)*

It was a compliment and a challenge. So I hope it provokes us to think seriously about the gap between this scribe and the kingdom. How close was he? What needed to change for him to come into the kingdom?

We find part of the answer in Jesus' quotation of two commandments about love. The scribe seems to assume that commandments fall into an order of importance or can be ranked. Jesus wisely ignores that false assumption.

---

15. Joseph was a secret follower, and perhaps Nicodemus (Mark 15:43; Luke 23:51; John 7:50–52; 19:38).

The commands to love God with everything you are and love your neighbor as yourself must not be separated. "On these two commandments depend the whole Law and the Prophets" (Matt. 22:40). John, the beloved disciple, had this love lesson so engrained that it became the central message of his first letter.[16] The scribe had studied the Old Testament so thoroughly that he understood God's heart and knew how important it was to love both God and fellow humans. He knew it was "much more than all burnt offerings and sacrifices" (Mark 12:33). What he understood showed his closeness to the kingdom.

However, understanding is not enough. The scribes were masters at learning Scripture. They were the legal experts, the law professors of that time. Their linguistic and theological skills were unsurpassed. But the process of studying Scripture is not what matters most; what matters is whether the study feeds a relationship with God or an oversized brain. It seems that our friendly scribe hadn't graduated to a relationship yet.

Perhaps one reason was the group he belonged to. The Pharisees with him had pushed the scribe forward to use his expertise to test Jesus (Matt. 22:34–35). They reckoned their role was that of guardians of orthodox Jewish religion, the ones who knew how to prepare Israel for the Messiah—and how to recognize a false one. Their position was respected and privileged. Society gladly gave them the best seats in the synagogues, and they expected the same at the banquets (Mark 12:38–39). It's hard to give up one's friends. And honor and respect feel so good. Do any of us question whether we really deserve them?

Jesus said some harsh words to these leaders. "Woe to you, scribes and Pharisees, hypocrites, because you shut off the kingdom of heaven from men; for you do not enter in yourselves, nor do you allow those who are entering to go in" (Matt. 23:13). Picture self-appointed bouncers at heaven's door.

Around us are religious systems built largely on study and expertise and supported by communities that find it easier to follow leaders as proxies than to pursue Jesus for themselves. Beware of those who are unable or unwilling

---

16. 1 John 2:9–10; 3:23; 4:7–8, 11, 20–21.

to jump the gap between knowing about God and a relationship with Him that overflows with practical love for others. Challenge them to jump but don't get stuck on their side of the gap.

Also around us are people who don't follow Jesus yet, but they share something of the heart of God. They're the ones who have compassion for the needy, fight against injustice and discrimination, share generously, and care more for spiritual and eternal things than for transient pleasures, to name a few traits. Do we recognize them and encourage them, "You are not far from the kingdom"?

What matters is not the nature or size of the gap but whether there is any movement in the right direction.

The ENTRY PASS

(Context: Luke 13:22–30.)

No one likes to be excluded from a valued group. People who suggest the exclusion of others are immediately unpopular and labeled as judgmental. John the Baptist offended the religious leaders when he gave his lesson about spiritual pedigree. "Do not suppose that you can say to yourselves, 'We have Abraham for our father,' for I say to you that God is able from these stones to raise up children to Abraham" (Matt. 3:9). Race, culture, and mere outward conformity to Christian practices count for nothing in the kingdom.

Jesus knew there would always be outsiders for whom the kingdom remains a closed mystery because their ears fail to hear in a way that changes their lives (Mark 4:1–12). The sad but irresistible fact is that not everyone will be included in the kingdom of God.

The gate is narrow. Locals who had dined with Him or heard His teaching thought their connections entitled them to flash a special access pass; they would be shocked when the head of the house refuses to open the door. *"I do not know where you are from; depart from me, all you evildoers"* (Luke 13:27). Association counts for nothing, and God does not entertain evil. Jesus said that many Jews, who considered themselves "sons of the kingdom," would be left out while many non-Jews would enter at the great reversal of last for first (Matt. 8:11–12; 21:33–44; Luke 13:30).

What's that reversal about? Religious eyes saw tax-gatherers and harlots as the scum of the earth of the day. But Jesus said they would enter the kingdom more easily than religious leaders because they are more inclined to act on their belief and do the Father's will (Matt. 21:31). Once there, they do not remain as they are; by definition, they obey and change. Tax-gatherers stop their covetous extortion; harlots abstain from lust and promiscuity. They are examples of those who humbly fall on the Stone, get broken, but receive new lives built from the fragments—better than being crushed and scattered like dust, eh! (Matt. 21:44)

It's not only those who display outward religion but lack righteousness who get left out (Matt. 5:20). General unrighteousness (1 Cor. 6:9–10; Gal. 5:21; Eph. 5:5); dismissing God's commands (Matt. 5:19; 7:21); an inability to let go of possessions and care for the needy (Matt. 19:23; 25:31–46; Mark 10:17–25; Luke 18:18–25); failing to stay alert and prepared (Matt. 25:1–13); or simply shrugging off the invitation because other things seem more pressing (Luke 9:59–62; 14:15–24)—there are so many reasons why people will find the entrance shut. There's only one way to get in.

A Roman centurion held a valid pass—faith. Jesus noted his simple willingness to trust His authority to heal and remarked that He had seen no faith like it in Israel. Faith would qualify multitudes; unbelief would exclude many who expected to be included (Matt. 8:5–13; Luke 7:1–10). For anyone to trust in Jesus' sacrificial death for salvation requires faith. That's what the blood-washed robes of Revelation 7:14 are about (and perhaps the appropriate attire of Matthew 22:1–14). Faith counts for righteousness, as it did with Abraham, the father of faith (Rom. 4:3–16). Faith unites the kingdom of priests from every tribe, tongue, people, and nation who reign with God. It sweeps away the selective genetic boundaries of the scribes and Pharisees (Rev. 5:9–10).

Everyone has an invitation and directions; not everyone chooses faith. James singled out one group as more likely to possess faith and enter the kingdom—the poor (Jas. 2:5 and compare Matt. 5:3 with Luke 6:20). Maybe it helps to have less of those clingy possessions that stifle faith. Perhaps they are so used to filling the role of servants that they more readily qualify for the reversal of last and first (Mark 9:35).

Whether we are rich or poor, the challenge to exercise faith is serious. Faith results in action. Faith motivates people to obey God, live righteously, keep a loose hold on possessions, and care for others. Faith births a kingdom lifestyle here on earth and keeps us alert and prepared to inherit the completed kingdom in the future. Accept no substitutes.

The
INVITATION

(Context: Luke 14:1–24.)

It must have been a strange and uncomfortable dinner party. Jesus sometimes ate with religious leaders, but His host on this Sabbath seemed hostile. Perhaps the man with dropsy had gate-crashed the meal to meet Jesus. Or was it a set-up? We will never know. Although the man was conspicuous in the Pharisee's house, he never stayed for dinner once he was healed. The religious leaders were certainly watching to see what Jesus would do. Jesus watched them too. Later, Jesus noted how they had subtly maneuvered to the best seats. Finally, He advised His host to alter the guest list next time. Invite people who can't return the favor—maybe even a man with dropsy. If you can believe it, the rewards for that are out of this world.

Another guest overheard Jesus' recommendation to include poor, crippled, lame, and blind people. His comment is interesting:

Blessed is everyone who shall eat bread in the kingdom of God.
(Luke 14:15)

At first, it sounds like an affirmation of Jesus' teaching. Or was the guest being cynical, sneering at the idea of a kingdom so lacking in principles that it readily included blemished people? It is indeed a blessing to be a subject of the kingdom of God, but the comment prompted a parable with a sad warning (Luke 14:16–24).

Most people relish an invitation to a banquet. So the story surprises us when the slave goes out to tell the guests everything is ready, but they all begin making excuses. You know: pressing business, shopping trips, new toys, investment opportunities, relationship priorities—things we can all relate to. Naturally, the host was upset. All that food! So, "waste not, want not," he sent the slave out to gather the poor, crippled, lame, and blind. When there was still room, he searched high and low, compelling everyone he could find to come to the feast. At last, the house was filled. But the original invitees wouldn't even smell the food.

It is easy to correctly comment that being part of the kingdom is wonderful (religion often says nice things). But to go beyond being trite or religious requires us to realize the value of the invitation, sweep our lives clear of all conflicting engagements, and simply show up.

The PEARL TRADER

(Context: Matthew 13:44–46.)

God's kingdom is like a trader seeking fine pearls. Upon finding one pearl of great value, he liquidated his assets and bought it.
(Matthew 13:45–46. My paraphrase.)

The pearl trader knew his business. He had studied pearls, gained experience in the markets of the Middle East, and learned to recognize the best. His life revolved around pearls. He traveled almost constantly, rarely spending more than a few nights at home. He knew how to trade: buy low, sell high, cut losses, and invest in pearls that would appreciate and had a market. Passage on ships, inns along the way, wining and dining suppliers and buyers; they were all tax deductions from his profit. What remained after covering family living expenses was reinvested in his search for the best.

I used to think that Jesus' parables of the treasure (the men got excited about buried treasure) and the pearl (the ladies' eyes lit up) were simply about the value of the kingdom of God. Certainly that's part of the lesson; it's so valuable that it costs us everything we have—our entire life. There are no Black Friday sales; it will never be reduced to clear. If we fail to pay full price, we receive a cheap imitation, often a religious substitute for the real thing.

However, we can't buy a place in the kingdom as though it's an exotic timeshare. It's not about a financial transaction. There is a better way to understand its value—the extent to which we are willing to exchange what we already have for it. The men in the parables sold all they had to acquire the treasure and the pearl. Their life goal was to obtain the most precious thing possible. (And surely the cultural assumption was that their extended family and friends would get a share.) For us, it might be giving up bad things or removing a clutter of harmless things, but it's about making space for God. So, what do we have that we could exchange? Our list probably looks something like this:

- The house with its furniture, decorations, outbuildings, land, and those beautiful flowering shrubs.
- Our toys and tools.
- Those memorabilia and family heirlooms.
- Investments.
- Perhaps a business.
- Relationships.

The list represents securities, comforts, conveniences, luxuries, status symbols, and even our identity. Life is not things. Nevertheless, think about how many of our activities are geared to supporting, protecting, or maintaining the list that, in part, defines us. Does God expect us to liquidate everything we have and, in some mystical way, exchange it all for His kingdom? How far should we stretch Jesus' parables?

Only when we understand what God's kingdom looks like on earth, can we grasp what exchanging everything we have means. Jesus invites His listeners to put themselves in the place of the pearl dealer. That man was focused. He worked to live, *and* he lived to work. Jesus wasn't talking about becoming homeless and penniless just to hold a priceless pearl; He was talking about aligning everything with the kingdom. Are we willing to relinquish whatever possessions and activities do not serve kingdom purposes to make room for things that do?[17]

---

17. Matt. 16:24–26; 19:12 talk of other sacrifices.

Jesus said, "Seek first the kingdom of God and His righteousness." He explained that our Father will supply everything we need to do His business. We are told to love the Lord our God with all our heart, mind, and strength because the King and His kingdom are the inseparable, priceless treasure. Gaining a relationship with Him and joining His kingdom business (all expenses paid) ... there's nothing like it.

LIVING IT

GOD'S LOVE LANGUAGE

(Context: Matthew 21:23–32.)

Don't rejoice too much when people adopt standards that are outwardly "Christian." The riskiest society for Jesus' followers to live in is one clothed with values that are close to biblical values, whether it uses the term "Christian" or not. God's kingdom ways are easy to swallow, but when a culture's values are close to the kingdom's, they are hard to digest. What do I mean? Simply that Jesus does not make pacts with people just because they like some of His values; He requires submission and obedience. Accepting Jesus and His values is easy if we agree with Him in those areas, but surrendering to Him is hard if we want a relationship based only on our ready agreement. If we don't listen and obey, our spiritual growth remains stunted.

Sometimes the religious leaders came close to agreeing with Jesus (Mark 12:28–34). They dined with Him and could mouth their blessings (Luke 14:1–24). But remember whose schemes got Him executed. One of Jesus' parables starred a father and two sons, the first of which represented those religious leaders. When the father asked the first son to work in the vineyard, he agreed, but never showed up. However, the second, who refused at first, later felt bad and set to work.

"Which of the two did the will of his father?" [The religious leaders] said, "The latter." Jesus said to them, "Truly I say to you that the

63

tax-gatherers and harlots will get into the kingdom of God before you. For John [the Baptist] came to you in the way of righteousness and you did not believe him, but the tax-gatherers and harlots did believe him; and you, seeing this, did not even feel remorse afterward so as to believe him." (Matthew 21:31–32. See also Matthew 7:21.)

Agreement and belief are good starts, but they must lead somewhere. Tax-gatherers and harlots changed when they heard John and Jesus.

Certainly, God accepts the simplest of worship: shepherds racing to a baby, magi braving hundreds of miles of desert to bow with precious gifts, the clink of two mites in the offering. True worship begins with humility and recognizing who He is—and that He is trustworthy and loving. To become a disciple as well as a worshipper requires listening and obediently following Him. Following is never completed by a single decision; an ongoing series of decisions sustains it. The closer we get to Him, the more we discover about Him, and an ever-deepening response is evoked.

Jesus frequently emphasized obedience. David and Paul Watson point out that obedience is how God spells "love."[18] It is how we best express our love to Him—His love language, if you like.[19] If "obedience" sounds too serious for our ears, that's probably because we associate it with discipline, performance, and punishment. In the kingdom, it works differently. Like any king, God calls His subjects to submit, but He does it for our good. Our obedience isn't about God's royal ego; it leads to what is best for us. We love God because we know His love for us is wrapped up in what He calls us to obey.

We must never separate the kingdom of God from the kingship of God. To receive more of the kingdom, we must welcome the increasing rule of the King in our lives.

---

18. David L. Watson and Paul D. Watson, *Contagious Disciple Making*, (Thomas Nelson, 2014), 45.
19. John 14:15–24; 1 John 5:2–3.

LEARNING *to* BREATHE AIR *and* FLY

(Context: Matthew 13:24–50; Mark 4:26–29. Parallels: Mark 4:30–32; Luke 13:18–21.)

Being realistic is considered a virtue. But what is reality? It depends on perspective. And opinions about reality are as inflexible as the system in which we live is closed. A fish thinks that the idea of a life in anything but water is absurd. But a caterpillar might have an inkling that to flutter by flowers and sip nectar all day is a valid dream. Jesus spoke to caterpillars and fish.

When we make a statement such as, "A is like B," the two items resemble each other or have some correspondence. But whenever Jesus said, "the kingdom of God is like," the parable that follows rarely fits that general rule.[20] How can the kingdom be "like" ten virgins or a fishing net with its slimy, flopping haul? When we analyze them, none of these parables illustrate the fully fledged kingdom. Jesus was talking about its transition from His time to its fullness and how people can receive or enter it. When the kingdom has arrived on earth as it is in heaven, there will be no mixture, and no need for mercy, forgiveness, or preparedness. So, presumably, Jesus meant, "during this transitional age, this is how the King runs His kingdom," or, "this attitude

----

20. Eleven parables in which Jesus said the equivalent of, "the kingdom is like," are in Matthew with just two parallels in Luke and a twelfth in Mark 4:26–29 that is similar. The leaven, seed, and treasure are easiest to liken to the kingdom because they simply illustrate its growth and value.

is necessary for kingdom life." His kingdom is different from our world; it's an enigma to human caterpillars, and especially fish.

Jesus' six parables of the kingdom in Matthew 13 are arranged in pairs. The tares and the dragnet form bookends for the other four: the mustard seed and leaven illustrate kingdom growth,[21] the hidden treasure and the pearl speak of its value.[22] Comparing the kingdom to a field that an enemy contaminated with weed seeds sketches the timeline for the kingdom. Until the end of the age, the crop and tares grow together. Then, the tares are ripped up and burnt. The parable of the dragnet full of various fish is a similar idea. Our world says that tidy monocultures of waving harvests or the tastiest, grill-ready catches are best for successful enterprises; God's kingdom does not develop like that. We must be patient and tolerate the mixture, trusting that He will remove contaminants justly in the end. Patient, because the timing is unknown.

In our systems, bigger and faster often seem better. Heaven's small beginnings are easy to despise, just like the tablespoon of yeast that I use for my pizza dough, or the tiny mustard seed that would vanish with a sneeze. Patient cooks and cultivators discover that little things can grow huge with time; people like them can receive God's kingdom more easily than others.

We want our cake and we want to eat it. Priceless treasures are nice additions to a collection—a great way to diversify or hedge investments. But to sell everything to get a pearl or buried treasure! That's risky—not something a financial advisor would recommend. However, Jesus taught total buy-in.

Matthew 18:21–35. We find bitterness easy and forgiveness hard. Most of the world thinks Peter was generous when he suggested forgiving someone seven times; it might expose him to abuse. Jesus upped it to four hundred and ninety and then portrayed the kingdom as an institution of lavish mercy and forgiveness. Only unforgiving people are denied them.

Matthew 20:1–16. Apart from mercy and forgiveness, compassion and generosity marked a vineyard owner in another story. We hold fairness as a high standard, but our idea of fairness often doesn't stretch much beyond me

---

21. Mark's parable of the seed that grows automatically is similar.
22. Perhaps one of each for men and women in His audience.

and mine, or exist beyond our recliner. In our world, we are conditioned to a shortage "reality," so rations and self-serving are the rule. In a kingdom of abundance, fairness includes consideration and generosity toward everyone.

Matthew 22:1–14. Earthly kingdoms hide human flaws behind fairy-tale behavior, pretending "reality" is better than it is. Almost everyone who gets an invitation to a leader's palace drops everything to attend, sporting smart, new clothes and brushed etiquette. Jesus was truly realistic; He knew that, on earth, few people take God seriously. They shrug off His invitations and even abuse His servants. The "realities" of our social and business priorities count as valid excuses. However, worthiness is not marked by being on the guest list but by showing up to the feast with the right covering. Worthiness requires taking the higher reality seriously.

Matthew 25:1–13. We like to lower the bar and give ourselves a break. We think it is fairest to give plenty of notice and reminders about important events. "Be real. We're busy and tired people!" And prudence is boring. Not so heaven. Those who remain alert and prepared will enter God's kingdom; their focus demonstrates faith that the unseen kingdom reality really is approaching.

Matthew 25:14–30. Again, Jesus urged investment. Whether it was talents or minas (Luke 19:11–27), the characters in the stories were rewarded for multiplying them or punished for sitting on them. The master seemed hard or strict because he expected returns from nowhere. It might appear unreasonable to us, but that's the reality of God's kingdom. The Father, who gladly gives the kingdom (Luke 12:32), guarantees returns on our investments—so invest!

To live in the reality that all twelve of these parables illustrate requires faith—faith that the truths and values described are more real than our experiences to date. The character of God undergirds them. They are the best for us because they are how God designed us to live from the beginning. It's faith in that reality that enables us to try them and, by doing so, bring more of heaven to earth. By faith, caterpillars become butterflies and fish learn to breathe air.

A PACKAGE DEAL

(Context: Ephesians 5:1–14.)

There's cheese, and there's cheese. I asked an international student if he knew what cheese was, and he said, "Oh, yes. It's what they put on burgers." He meant the processed, artificially colored and preserved cheese slices that share many characteristics of soft rubber. Anne Saxelby knew cheese.[23] She sold artisan cheeses from her stall in New York. Her suppliers crafted fine cheeses using raw milk from their herds of sheep, goats, or cows, blending flavors subtly influenced by seasonal changes in the pastures, and the flowers that grew among the grasses. Well, there are Christians, and there are Christians, too.[24]

Words are cheap—even the word "Christian." Be wary of anyone who recites Scripture or labels themself "Christian" to validate themself or to make an argument, unless they and their argument are in line with God. The devil tried it to test Jesus. After Jesus resisted him twice by quoting from Deuteronomy, the devil copied His approach and appealed to the authority of Psalm 91:11–12 to test Jesus a third time (Luke 4:9–12). Jesus was not persuaded; He knew that any verse outside the context of the will and ways of God is just cheap words.

---

23. *The Economist*, October 30, 2021, 90.

24. This is one of the reasons that I prefer to call myself a follower or disciple of Jesus, though I am sure the biblical definition of "Christian" still applies.

Paul makes it clear that, when it comes to "being a Christian," empty words are not enough. Kingdom subjects are children of God, and saints—set apart to live differently.[25] There is an open invitation to God's kingdom, but His family has standards and is expected to imitate Him.

Do not let immorality or any impurity or greed even be named among you, as is proper among saints; and there must be no filthiness and silly talk, or coarse jesting, which are not fitting, but rather giving of thanks. For this you know with certainty, that no immoral or impure person or covetous man, who is an idolater, has an inheritance in the kingdom of Christ and God. Let no one deceive you with empty words, for because of these things the wrath of God comes upon the sons of disobedience. Therefore do not be partakers with them; for you were formerly darkness, but now you are light in the Lord; walk as children of light. (Ephesians 5:3–8[26])

Later, Paul talks more about light. "All things become visible when they are exposed by the light, for everything that becomes visible is light" (Eph. 5:13–14). What Jesus does for us, in a nutshell, is to shine on us, exposing, then bleaching, our sin. We come alive. We become His radiant light for others, exposing and correcting their deeds of darkness.

Right from the early days, when God blessed Abraham, it was so that He and Israel could be a blessing to the nations (Gen. 12:1–3). The prophets repeatedly called the Jews to a lifestyle appropriate to their being people of God. To enjoy the blessings and spread the blessings, we have to live the life-style. It's a package deal; it always has been.

---

25. The word "saint" relates to the word "holy," which means "set apart." The process by which followers of Jesus become saints is sanctification, which is another related word (1 Cor. 6:11).

26. See also 1 Corinthians 6:9–10; 1 Thess. 2:12.

LIVING *a* GODLESS LIFE *in a* GODLESS KINGDOM

(Context: Daniel 1:1–21.)

I sympathize with Christians who struggle to distinguish a kingdom lifestyle from the lifestyle of the world. When society grants religious freedom and holds many healthy values, the distinctions blur. The color contrasts fade with proximity. We grow up fully immersed in our native culture. Normal seems natural—and mostly good. Saintly unbelievers are commonplace, and we all know believers who shrug off Christian behavioral expectations as tedious, outdated, or legalistic. "Be nice and be happy." "Live and let live." They are the bland, new, one-size-fits-all mottoes.

So, what are the standards of a kingdom lifestyle, and what is unnecessary legalism or stale tradition? It helps to read about the lives of biblical people of faith. From a distance of two millennia or more, the contrast between the world and the kingdom of God is easier to see. Take Daniel and his friends. They lived a godly life in a godless kingdom. How did they do it?

We meet them in Babylonian exile, robbed of freedom and forced into a royal finishing school. Babylon tried to squeeze godly life and noble identity out of them—re-educating them, providing food from the royal kitchen, putting their natural abilities into foreign service, and assigning pagan names. Daniel became Belteshazzar. (Daniel 1:1–7)

It sounds okay (especially the food). They might have been very happy, but they made a dangerous stand—against the food. Dissenting prisoners of war could have been dispatched with a click of the royal fingers. But God granted favor; Daniel and his friends were spared the defiling diet.

> *Daniel made up his mind that he would not defile himself with the king's choice food or with the wine which he drank; so he sought permission from the commander of the officials that he might not defile himself. Now God granted Daniel favor and compassion in the sight of the commander of the officials, and the commander of the officials said to Daniel, "I am afraid of my lord the king, who has appointed your food and your drink; for why should he see your faces looking more haggard than the youths who are your own age? Then you would make me forfeit my head to the king." But Daniel said to the overseer whom the commander of the officials had appointed over Daniel, Hananiah, Mishael and Azariah, "Please test your servants for ten days, and let us be given some vegetables to eat and water to drink. Then let our appearance be observed in your presence and the appearance of the youths who are eating the king's choice food; and deal with your servants according to what you see." (Daniel 1:8–13)*

Daniel and his friends became models of healthy eating and came top of their class. They entered royal service and excelled. It was the first of three tests. He and his friends also refused to worship Nebuchadnezzar's image (Dan. 3), and Daniel continued to petition God despite King Darius' stern decree banning prayer (Dan. 6).

Instead of losing their identity and their heads, the men flourished. Their identities remained intact (notice that the book calls them by their Hebrew names, not their Babylonian ones) and they kept their anointing. As they honored God, He gave them favor. They did serve the pagan kingdom using their God-given gifts, but without compromise. Daniel pointed the Babylonian kings beyond their realms to God's kingdom. Three kings of Babylon came to respect God because of Daniel.

Daniel and his friends show us how to live a kingdom lifestyle in a lost world. There should be no compromise in three areas:

- Worship belongs to God alone.
- Prayer—our communication with God. Are you going elsewhere for guidance, provision, or deliverance?
- God's instructions. Dietary laws found in Scripture distinguished the Jewish life. Although Jesus changed the focus of the Christian life away from laws, the kingdom lifestyle still has standards.

What motivated Daniel to risk his life for these three things? Perhaps His name provides a clue. "Daniel" means "God is my judge." As the Judge, God does not simply punish disobedience; he also rewards loyalty. Daniel remained conscious that God saw everything he did and would bring a just reward. That hasn't changed.

BOOKLETS
of BLESSINGS

(Context: Matthew 5:1–12. Parallel: Luke 6:20–26.)

Imagine the Beatitudes of Matthew 5:3–12 as booklets on a library shelf. The first and last are like bookends indicating what this section of the library shelf is about—access to, or possession of, the kingdom of heaven.[27] In the Beatitudes, Jesus seems to say two connected things: "Those who already live the way I am describing are ripe for the kingdom." Also: "If you live this way, you will find yourself in the kingdom."

Eight "blesseds" are followed by a ninth that seems to expand on the eighth. The first and eighth specifically state possession of, or access to, the kingdom. The ninth promises a reward in heaven. Let's skim through the booklets:

Blessed are the poor in spirit, for theirs is the kingdom of heaven. Material poverty in needy Galilee meant destitution. Human spirits, with no other life source (or master, Matt. 6:24), are like a vacuum ready to suck up life, a blank canvas inviting color and design. The kingdom most easily belongs to the poor in spiritual and material things (James 2:5).

---

27. In fact, the whole Sermon on the Mount is about "entry" to that kingdom (Matthew 7:21) or life in it. The following footnotes provide specific examples of expansions on the Beatitudes within the sermon.

Blessed are those who mourn, for they shall be comforted. The single Greek word "shall be comforted" has the same root as "the Comforter," which is used of the Holy Spirit. The Spirit of God is the One who comes alongside, not just to say, "There, there, it will be alright," but to provide invigorating comfort—His presence and help. There is comfort in the kingdom because God is present.

Blessed are the [gentle/humble/meek], for they shall inherit the earth. There is a Hebrew expression, *ha'arets*, meaning "the land." For Jews, it meant more than territory; their identity, dignity, and destiny were tied to it. Gentle, humble, or meek people will receive their promised inheritance from God because He exalts the humble and gives them grace.[28]

Those who hunger and thirst for righteousness … shall be satisfied. This speaks of a craving for more than personal righteousness; it includes a longing for it in the world. Of course those who are desperate for righteousness will be satisfied—righteousness is an essence of the kingdom. Jesus came to impart righteousness to those who accept Him. His righteousness runs deeper than the skin-deep religious kind (Matt. 5:20).

The merciful … shall receive mercy. Like comfort and righteousness, mercy is in the King's nature. Those who display His character receive it back. God will never be out-given.[29]

The pure in heart … shall see God. Impurities divert our spiritual eyes or obscure our view of God. As King, He is the center of the kingdom. Pure hearts are crystal clear, focused only on Him.[30]

Peacemakers … shall be called sons of God. Being a "son of" someone or something means sharing the same DNA and character. Again, there may be a Hebrew concept behind this. "Peace" is *shalom*. *Shalom* means more than the absence of strife; it is wellbeing and wholeness. Peacemakers don't just

---

28. The gentle/humble/meek shun anger and retaliation; they love their enemies (Matt. 5:38–44) and deal with the log in their own eyes (Matt. 7:1–5).

29. The merciful do not retaliate (Matt. 5:38–48).

30. The pure in heart amputate anything that leads them astray (Matt. 5:29–30). Their speech is straightforward (Matt. 5:37).

prevent or resolve conflict; they bring health and wholeness. That's what the Father does; peacemakers reflect Him.[31]

Blessed are those who have been persecuted for the sake of righteousness, for theirs is the kingdom of heaven. No one goes through persecution unless they are stubbornly committed to whatever their persecutor hates. This line tells of hunger for rightness in the eyes of God, at any price.[32]

The ninth Beatitude continues the thought of the eighth, but Jesus no longer talks about a third party; He speaks to "you" and what you do "on account of" Him.[33] *Blessed are you when men cast insults at you, and persecute you, and say all kinds of evil against you falsely, on account of Me. Rejoice, and be glad, for your reward in heaven is great, for so they persecuted the prophets who were before you.* Commitment to Jesus will be tested by various degrees of opposition. The prophets were persecuted primarily because they called for kingdom living on earth—the righteous ways of God in every aspect of life. Persecution is probably the ultimate test of kingdom life. Children of God respond in an opposite spirit, with love and prayer for their enemies (Matt. 5:38–45).

---

31. Peacemakers go beyond passive peacekeeping; they reconcile with their brother and opponent and show marital faithfulness (Matt. 5:23–26). They love their enemies and forgive their debtors (Matt. 5:38–44; 6:12).

32. Much of the rest of the Sermon on the Mount is about practical righteousness. Matt. 5:20 is expanded in the rest of chapter five and summarized at 5:48. Matt. 6:1–18 talks about focusing on the Father, not men. Matt. 6:33 again urges us to seek righteousness.

33. This continues through the rest of the sermon.

INVESTMENT ADVICE

(Context: Acts 14:8–28.)

Every few years, investments take a plunge. Anyone holding assets when the rallying music stops is at the top of a financial rollercoaster. Their heart seems to be in their mouth, and their hair is tugged as their net worth plummets. Behind every silent (or vocal) scream are questions like, "How long will this last?" "Will it be a soft landing?" "Will I ever recover?"

There are times when life in the kingdom of God seems to take turns like that. Once, angry Jews dragged Paul's limp body out of Lystra, thinking he was dead. But he regained consciousness and returned with Barnabus, *"strengthening the souls of the disciples, encouraging them to continue in the faith, and saying, 'Through many tribulations we must enter the kingdom of God.'"* (Acts 14:22)

Was Paul a pessimist to say such a thing? No. You see, he understood the conflict between God's kingdom and the world's ways. He knew things could get tough. He knew it would take faith to endure. Jesus didn't mince His words either (though we often miss His point). If anyone wishes to follow Him, they must be prepared to be treated as a rebel and face whatever consequences their society decides to impose on them for sticking out (Matt. 16:24–26). For Jesus, that was crucifixion.

In a place where all we know of physical persecution for faith in Jesus is stories from other parts of the world, it's hard to relate to the topic. No one has done more than laugh at me. But I have international friends who have been in prison. Another friend's father tried to kill him for leaving the Hindu faith to follow Jesus. Several make daily choices about how much to share with friends or post on social media because they are breaking the law and risking their careers. For all of them (and us in smaller ways), it's a choice between obediently serving Jesus and staying comfortable. It would have been understandable for Paul to slink past Lystra; he returned because Jesus had called him to bear His name to the Gentiles and had warned him of suffering (Acts 9:15-16).

The warning is essential because, when persecution happens, it shows that Jesus knew what He was talking about and that we're still on course. If He's right about the path, He will be right about the glory and the reward too. Although Jesus gave few details about the reward, we know it's a place of honor in His kingdom (Matt. 5:10-12; Luke 22:28-30).

Paul had weighed potential suffering against the certain reward and chosen to live as an ambassador, sharing good news about the kingdom to a hostile world. The book of Acts tells that story. Society has programmed us to think of any imprisonment as shameful; it's not when it's for Jesus. Paul spent years under guard while the Roman legal machinery processed him. He viewed each step of the way as an opportunity to share his hope with fellow prisoners, accusers, and authorities. Two years of house arrest on Caesar's doorstep was a gift to him; it fulfilled a promise that God had given years earlier (Acts 19:8; 20:25; 23:11; 28:23, 30-31). Persecution was common for Peter and other apostles too. After being imprisoned and flogged, they rejoiced that they were found worthy to suffer for Jesus (Acts 5:40-42; 12:1-3. See also 2 Thess. 1:4-5; Rev. 1:9). All of them had counted the cost and decided that it was worth risking their lives to serve Jesus.

Anyone who is prepared to suffer for Jesus has made an investment decision. Time, freedom, health, relationships, career, and even life itself are put at risk because the reward is considered both precious and certain. Jesus was looking for that kind of faith in two would-be followers (Luke 9:59-62). He emphasized it in a story about investment told in slightly different ways (Matt. 25:14-30; Luke 19:11-27). The message was the same: worthy servants do whatever they can to maximize the return on what the master entrusts to them. He rewards good and faithful servants but punishes risk-averse servants who fail to invest.

Paul, Peter, and others are examples of investing well. Even when they were not being ill-treated, they focused their resources and time on spreading the good news of the kingdom. To follow their example, we must be clear about the trustworthiness of Jesus' claims and promises and start taking risks for Him. The soundest advice about investing in the kingdom of God will always be "buy and hold." But be prepared for some unnerving downturns.

FRIENDS
and FAMILY

(Context: Matthew 12:46–50; Luke 14:25–26. Parallels: Mark 3:31–35; Luke 8:19–21.)

In 1820, Thomas Jefferson produced a moral code of Jesus. Using a razor and glue, he cut and pasted passages from the four Gospels into chronological order. However, he excluded any mention of miracles and ended with the sealing of Jesus' tomb. Jefferson did not believe in God's supernatural involvement in this world. His Jesus was merely a great and good teacher. *The Life and Morals of Jesus of Nazareth* supported his own opinions.[34]

Was Thomas Jefferson so unusual? Aren't we all tempted to do our own "cut and paste" exercises in our minds, conversations, and behavior? What do we do with those statements in the Bible that grate against our preferences or experiences? We are born into self-rule. The Bible is bound to challenge us because it points to a changed life under the rule of a new King. Consider Jesus' statements about friends and family as an example. Anyone with no exposure to the teachings of Jesus might well be shocked and run for the scissors:

> *Someone said to Him, "Behold, Your mother and Your brothers are standing outside seeking to speak to You." But Jesus answered the one who was telling Him and said, "Who is My mother and who are*

---

34. *https://en.wikipedia.org/wiki/Jefferson_Bible.*

My brothers?" And stretching out His hand toward His disciples, He said, "Behold My mother and My brothers! For whoever does the will of My Father who is in heaven, he is My brother and sister and mother." (Matthew 12:47–50. See too Luke 11:27–28.)

"If anyone comes to Me, and does not hate his own father and mother and wife and children and brothers and sisters, yes, and even his own life, he cannot be My disciple. (Luke 14:26. See too Matthew 10:37.)

You are My friends if you do what I command you. No longer do I call you slaves, for the slave does not know what his master is doing; but I have called you friends, for all things that I have heard from My Father I have made known to you. (John 15:14–15)

Let's be clear, Jesus did *not* say that friends and family are bad and are not recognized in His kingdom. He did *not* mean we are to literally *hate* our family members. Rather, He used a Jewish way of speaking to tell His followers that love for Him must *surpass* our love for any other person or object, including our own lives. Faced with a choice, we should choose Him. Jesus' statement about family was a thinly veiled claim to sovereignty.

The new Sovereign stated a new way for life to work best. His kingdom family is not bounded by blood and marriage. The friends of the King are those who do what He commands. The door is open to everyone who chooses.

Now, if we think that obedience to Jesus' commands is impossibly daunting, then we assume that Jesus is pretty lonely. But when we explore Jesus' life and teachings more thoroughly, we find that the sticking point is giving up self-rule. His commands are straightforward after that. Obedience flows naturally when we trust and love Jesus (John 14:15).

But obedience can still sound like servitude, even if the master is a nice guy. Jesus corrected that falsehood. Slaves are kept in the dark about the

King's objectives; the King tells His friends what He is doing and entrusts kingdom business to them. Also, our Father provides all the resources we need to do His will.

The challenge to us is to rise above our small world of human relationships, love them, but make Jesus King, and live His way.

INTIMATE
ENCOUNTERS

Before you read this, do a little exercise. Think about the life and ministry of Jesus as we know it from the Gospels. Of course, He spent the most time with His family and His disciples. But beyond them, what were Jesus' most intimate encounters (based on the topic, time spent, and emotional content)?

Finished? How does your list compare to my top ones?

John 4	The promiscuous woman of Samaria.
John 8:1–11	An adulteress.
John 20:11–18	Mary Magdalene, clinging to Jesus when she met Him by His tomb.
John 11	Mary and Martha in their grief at Lazarus' death.
John 3:1–21	An evening with Nicodemus.
John 12:1–8	Mary with the nard.
Luke 19:1–10	Staying with Zaccheus.
Matt. 9:20–22	A woman with a hemorrhage.
Matt. 17:1–8	Peter, James, and John at the transfiguration.

Perhaps your list differs from mine, but I see an interesting pattern. Women head my list and, shocking as it seems, in two cases, the interactions mentioned their sexual relationships. Typical Christian teaching says that, outside of marriage, men and women should keep their distance and avoid intimate conversations. Jesus seems to have missed that teaching. So how do we respond to the pattern?

One answer is to make Jesus the exception. I.e., Jesus is the perfect Son of God; He could do whatever He wanted. However, we are told that He was *"tempted in all things as we are, yet without sin"* (Hebrews 4:15). Did Jesus resist temptation because He was special? That misses the point of the verse: Jesus is like us but still overcame temptation. So perhaps the women that He encountered were not tempting. Somehow, I doubt that they went around with sacks over their heads.

Doesn't this pattern of intimate encounters make a statement about our new life as children of God? Jesus valued women and treated them honorably, not as dispensable playthings or possessions. He cared enough to listen to their hearts. He could speak into their pain, shame, and confusion. He accepted their affection. His longer-standing relationships with women like Mary Magdalene were probably consistent with Paul's counsel to Timothy to treat *"the older women as mothers, and the younger women as sisters, in all purity"* (1 Timothy 5:2).

Jesus demonstrated kingdom behavior—the life we are inheriting. He was an example of how to have an intimate friendship without straying into an inappropriate relationship.

There are plenty of opportunities for today's men (and women) to do the same!

MAKING YOU-KNOW-WHO GREAT

(Context: Mark 10:35–45. Parallel: Matthew 20:20–28.)

We are so familiar with our lives that we often assume the kingdom runs the same way. Yet it is different. In western culture, we associate success with large numbers—people, dollars, acres, toys, awards, etc. We behave as though the kingdom runs democratically when, in fact, it is a benevolent monarchy. In much of the world, the expectation is for children to mature and become independent; spiritual maturity involves greater dependence on God. A negative example is a struggle some people have to know God as a good and intimate father when their earthly father was anything but that.

James and John assumed God's kingdom matched their experience in yet another area. They (Matthew says their mother) asked a favor of Jesus: special positions next to Jesus in His kingdom glory. Jesus' response shows that they were asking for authority as top rulers. The response of the other disciples suggests that James and John were simply quicker to ask for the favor (or they had a sharper mother).

Notice the contrast, in this case, between the kingdom of God and the world. James and John grew up in a world of political appointees who had connections but perhaps questionable merit. Maybe Jesus' kingdom would run that way. Jesus countered their assumption with two kingdom values—suffering and service.

Jesus said to them, "You do not know what you are asking for. Are you able to drink the cup that I drink, or to be baptized with the baptism with which I am baptized?" (Mark 10:38)

Jesus meant the cup and baptism of suffering and death. James and John sniffed, stiffened, and said they were able. Jesus said they would share those things, but kingdom positions were not His to assign. When the other disciples became indignant, Jesus gave a mini-lesson about greatness.

"Whoever wishes to be great among you shall be your servant; and whoever wishes to be first among you shall be slave of all. For even the Son of Man did not come to be served, but to serve, and to give His life a ransom for many." (Mark 10:43–45)

That reminds us of two occasions when Jesus told His followers that a slave or disciple is not greater than his master (not exempt from the hard things the Master faced): When He washed their feet as an example, and when He warned them they would be hated and persecuted because Jesus-followers belong to a counter-kingdom (Matt. 10:24; John 13:12–17; 15:18–21). Jesus was clear: the kingdom lifestyle includes service and suffering.

Jesus' exemplary life shows that we cannot just study serving and suffering, contribute a token of each for some practical examination, and then move on to a new module in our spiritual education. Service flowed regularly from Jesus; hatred and misunderstanding were frequent. Life is full of situations where we must re-apply the values so they become increasingly engrained in our lives.

REVERSING FIRST *and* LAST

(Context: Matthew 19:16–20:16. Parallels: Mark 10:17–31; Luke 18:18–30.)

What's in it for me? It's a common question. We are used to a world that pays wages for work and uses rewards to motivate people to excel. A conversation between Jesus and a wealthy young man set Peter questioning along the same lines.

In answer to the young man's inquiry about obtaining eternal life, Jesus had told him to liquidate his possessions, give the money to the poor, and follow Him. The young man was unwilling to make the sacrifice. Peter, who had left his fishing business, home, and family to follow Jesus, wanted to know, "What then will there be for us?" (Matt. 19:27). Presumably, he expected Jesus to expand upon the rewards of eternal life in the kingdom of God (Matt. 19:16, 24). And Jesus did just that; He promised authority and eternal life but also hundredfold returns on what they had sacrificed, even in this life (Mark 10:30). So far, so good. But then Jesus took everyone by surprise—including us.

> *"Many who are first will be last; and the last, first. For the kingdom of heaven is like a landowner who went out early in the morning to hire laborers for his vineyard."* (Matthew 19:30–20:1)

Mark and Luke skip the vineyard parable; Matthew includes it as Jesus' illustration of how the kingdom reverses first and last. The fact that it starts a new chapter makes it easy to miss the connection, but chapters and verses were added long after the Bible was written.

The parable forces wrong-thinkers to rethink. Those who followed Jesus simply to hear His teaching, witness amazing miracles, or get a laugh as He silenced the religious leaders had to reconcile with a parable that spoke of hired laborers. The kingdom is like a business. There's work to do. But the King will pay whatever is right (Matt. 20:4). Naturally, those who work all day can expect a fair day's wage (Matt. 20:2).

But the shift in thinking continues. The landowner does the unexpected (pays those hired last first) and the unthinkable (pays the last a full day's wage). No wonder those who worked through the heat of a twelve-hour day grumbled. Like us (and Peter), they expected wages in proportion to work. It felt like bait and switch—give up everything only to be treated just like everyone else. It wasn't, but the kingdom of heaven sure is different. The King is not a cheat (He paid the agreed day's wage); He is generous (Matt. 20:9–16). And that forces yet another change in our thinking.

We must set aside the practices and standards we are accustomed to. In God's kingdom, rewards are not necessarily proportional to effort. The owner compensated the last laborers with a day's wage for their availability and because they needed that much to survive. Generosity[35] and compassion are high values in the kingdom. Also, because God's provision for our needs is unlimited, it is unnecessary to work extra to get more. There's no need to compete with each other either.

Although the New Testament mentions many things that God will reward, it reveals little about the *reward* except that it is life in the kingdom. The parables of the talents and minas even suggest that the reward for faithfulness is increased responsibility (Matt. 25:21, 23; Luke 19:17, 19).

All this points to a new kind of motivation in the kingdom of God. Eternal life in the kingdom is *the* fully satisfying reward because it revolves around our unhindered relationship with the King. Serving alongside King Jesus in His fruit-bearing business is reward enough: Experiencing His

---

35. Or "goodness." The word *agathos* simply means "good."

guidance, His multiplication and prospering of our tiny contributions, the joy of His presence, sharing the influence of His reign, knowing the security of His generous provision—these are the true rewards of followers, first and last.

SEEK FIRST
the KINGDOM

(Context: Matthew 6:9–13, 19–34. Parallels: Luke 11:2–13; 12:22–34.)

Is it any wonder that some people read the Gospels in a way that supports self-indulgence? So many of the stories in the Bible tell how God rescues, protects, heals, and provides for His children. It's easy to absorb the pattern and treat God primarily as our go-to in times of need. Only when we dig deeper into the teaching of Jesus does that simplistic view get challenged. He calls us to lay down our lives, be generous with our treasures, and accept suffering and persecution for the sake of His name. Jesus' Sermon on the Mount is a major source of correction. Consider these verses:

> *Pray then in this way: "Our Father who art in heaven, hallowed be Thy name. Thy kingdom come. Thy will be done on earth as it is in heaven. Give us this day our daily bread." (Matthew 6:9–11)*

> *Seek first His kingdom and His righteousness; and all these things shall be added to you. (Matthew 6:33)*

There are spoiled children and mature children. Don't misread the stories of God's lavish love and grace as encouragement for self-indulgence. Our heavenly Father lays a foundation of provision and protection in our lives because they are His nature. His care is universal (Matt. 5:45). His mercy and love are like a constant spring flowing to good and evil people alike, regardless of response. What we do with that flow is our choice. Will we go to the spring only when we feel a need, or will we press in to know the Source of the spring? Will we live by it and extend its flow by our practical love for others? Merciful miracles and provisions are signs of God's reality and demonstrate His care. They are a start, an invitation, but maturing includes developing a healthy balance between receiving kingdom blessings and spreading them.

If our relationship with God focuses on His blessings and help in need, it remains somewhat superficial. Experiencing God's constant abundance should lead us to overflow. Jesus received the Father's provision, protection, and guidance. From His deep sense of worth and security, He ministered to others. Intimacy in any relationship requires us to go beyond receiving; it develops as we share experiences and goals. When we make God's kingdom and the righteous lifestyle that accompanies it our priority, our relationship with Him deepens beyond the universal experience of His care. We live as children of God, like Jesus, junior partners in the family business. He supplies our needs so that we can extend His kingdom to others.

"Thy Kingdom Come," should never be a rote prayer. It should be the verbal expression of an entire life devoted to seeing the kingdom come.

EXTENDING IT

The
WAITERS

(Context: Luke 23:50-55. Parallels: Matthew 27:57-61; Mark 15:42-47; John 19:38-42.)

It took a while to sort out the confusion. Friends had just arrived at the airport and called to tell me which door they were at. I raced up to the curb outside Arrivals, but I could not see them. I called them back and a quick conversation suggested the problem. "Hey. Are you outside the Departures entrance?" I told them to come down the elevator to Arrivals. Then it was easy; I recognized them as they came through the door near where I had parked.

In Jesus' day, there was confusion about the kingdom of God. Prophets had given a sketchy outline, but it had been colored in with various ideas and desires. Some were as far from the truth as Arrivals is from Departures. Many people (especially those who had studied the subject) held their views so stubbornly that they rejected the kingdom as it came.

Joseph of Arimathea was an exception. Luke paints a mixed picture of Joseph. He was a member of the council of Jewish religious leaders, a good and righteous man. The council members were all priests (Pharisees or Sadducees) and mostly opposed to Jesus. Not Joseph. He clearly dissented when they condemned Jesus. He *"was waiting for the kingdom of God; [he] went to Pilate and asked for the body of Jesus. And he took it down and wrapped it in a linen cloth, and laid Him in a tomb cut into the rock, where no one had ever lain"* (Luke 23:50-53). It was his act of respect.

Waiting (*prosdechomai* in Greek) implies expectation, and a readiness to receive.[36] How could a Jewish religious leader, so steeped in Old Testament Law and Jewish tradition, balance his religion with an expectant desire for God's kingdom? Perhaps the answer is clear when the tradition is stripped away. For all the rules, rituals, and traditional ideas, the Jews had a high view of God. They knew He is good, powerful, and loyal to His people. Anyone who understood that an accurate view of the kingdom had to center on the King (rather than detached religious tradition) would easily get excited about living under God's rule.

Does it matter if our ideas of the kingdom are inaccurate? Not if we hold them loosely. Jesus gave us plenty of examples and teaching about kingdom lifestyle; the picture should be clear, if we pay attention and don't get distracted. Almost every teaching about the kingdom in the New Testament tells of the condition, attitude, and behavior of people in relationship with Him. So don't get carried away envisioning its organization, structure, and timing. Keep an open mind about the details. In the end, the best way to receive the kingdom is to grow close to the King. When we recognize Him, like friends at the airport, we will recognize His kingdom. It's coming all around us, though its fulness awaits the end of history.

Those who wait for the kingdom seek the King more than anything else. Practical needs do not distract because Father takes care of the seekers (Luke 12:31). The next verse suggests that some people want His kingdom so much that they are anxious that it may not come. Jesus reassures them that the Father has chosen gladly to *give* the kingdom (Luke 12:32). A few verses later, the same waiting word tells of the King's servants who remain alert for His return (Luke 12:36).

So, are our faith and desire focused on the kingdom of God? If you're like me, you want to be with other waiters: people who are focused and alert for the King and His increasing kingdom, not a religious substitute.

---

36. Simeon and the people that Anna shared the news with were also waiting (Luke 2:25, 38).

A GARDEN KINGDOM

Radishes. They're what come to mind when I think about seeds that sprout and grow easily. I worked on a vegetable farm for several summer breaks and we grew a lot. We'd scatter the seeds liberally on finely harrowed soil and within two weeks there would be a miniature forest of shoots on little red roots that had begun to swell. Jesus used a grain crop to illustrate a kingdom truth.

> *The kingdom of God is like a man who casts seed upon the soil and goes to bed at night and gets up by day, and the seed sprouts up and grows—how, he himself does not know. The soil produces crops by itself; first the blade, then the head, then the mature grain in the head. But when the crop permits, he immediately puts in the sickle, because the harvest has come. (Mark 4:26–29)*

Sounds easy, doesn't it? And that's where we take one of two mental paths concerning the kingdom. Most likely, we sift through our ideas about farming and note all the challenges involved. You know: late frosts, early droughts, bad seeds, soggy seeds, birds, bugs, and pesky deer. Then we blend them into our concept of the kingdom of God, and Jesus' little story wilts.

The other path is to take Jesus at His word. Jesus seems unhesitatingly optimistic. Be as liberal as you want with the seed. Sleep soundly—it's guaranteed to produce a harvest. When we think about it, this is not a new idea. Isaiah said God's government will increase forever, and His word will never fail to produce (Isa. 9:7; 55:10–13). Other kingdom parables talk of its surprising growth (Matt. 13:31–33; Mark 4:30–32; Luke 13:18–21). And we should never be anxious about the kingdom coming, because the Father has chosen gladly to give it to His little flock (Luke 12:32).

The path we choose depends on our faith and on how much we blend our ideas of reality with Jesus' bold and simple story. And choosing a path means taking action. In some ways, we are in the position of the unidentified man in the parable. If we act according to the story, we will scatter kingdom seed liberally and see a harvest. All around us, perhaps daily, are people and situations into which we can sow the truth, love, and power of God, just as Jesus did. All it takes is alertness to His leading and to their needs. We never see Jesus striving or being anxious. He never calculated the chances of offense, rejection, or acceptance. He did what was at hand, and soft hearts responded. Not everyone entered the kingdom; some delayed and, presumably, some never did enter. But Jesus sowed seeds and, after the Holy Spirit had filled His followers, the harvest began with thousands and continues to come in.

So, let's begin each day by saying to the King, "Father, I am ready to scatter and nurture your kingdom today. Show me how and where." Then take every opportunity to be like Jesus and watch the seeds grow where they can.

FAO Spies

I once had to sign an Official Secrets Act. My lips remain sealed about most of my work, but I will tell you that the information I had access to included nothing more sensitive than the number of bread rolls consumed by military units in a certain region. I worked in a rations office. So spies, don't bother trying to track or hack me.

The two spies that Joshua sent into Jericho brought back far more helpful intelligence. They discovered that the city was terrified of Israel and God. The Canaanites had heard the news about Israel's crushing victories over Egyptians and Amorites, and the miracles that God had done for Israel. According to inside information provided by agent Rahab, Jericho was braced for a beating.

> I know that the Lord has given you the land, and that the terror of you has fallen on us, and that all the inhabitants of the land have melted away before you. For we have heard how the Lord dried up the water of the Red Sea before you when you came out of Egypt, and what you did to the two kings of the Amorites who were beyond the Jordan, to Sihon and Og, whom you utterly destroyed. When we heard it, our hearts melted and no courage remained in any man any longer because of you; for the Lord your God, He is God in heaven above and on earth beneath. (Joshua 2:9–11)

Centuries earlier, God had planned to place Israel on a strip of land between the Mediterranean Sea and the Euphrates River. The nation was to be an instrument for spreading His kingdom worldwide. Whenever God commits to a plan, nothing can stop it. Even the melting of Canaanite hearts had been predicted forty years earlier when Israel stepped up from the Red Sea (Exodus 15:15). Canaan should have bowed to the unstoppable will of God.

Satan knows God's irresistible determination. The crushing defeat of sin and death on an old rugged cross still haunts him. Demons are astute theologians; they understand the truth and they tremble (James 2:19). But do you and I really know that they tremble? If the king of Jericho had captured Joshua's spies, the Israelites would never have understood Jericho's paralyzing fear. If the ruler of darkness can keep Jesus' followers in the dark, or silence them, then he preserves his hold. That is why Satan pursues anyone who recognizes the extent of Jesus' victory and who is in a position to proclaim that victory to others. But the truth is, he has already been defeated and has no hold on those who are in Christ.

Now that the secret is out, make sure that you keep reading the biblical intelligence reports about God's victory and His unswerving purposes. Get the truth about the condition of the enemy clear in your mind. Let that truth produce a new boldness, so you march into whatever God has called you to. Feed the information to as many people as you can, and battle in prayer for the spies who spread the good news to others.

The
OPEN SECRET

These days, important communications between embassy staff and government officials travel in diplomatic pouches or bags. The contents are legally immune from search and delay. They remain secret to foreign countries. Sometime around AD 33, a long-awaited "diplomatic bag" arrived in a hostile kingdom. It contained the mystery of the gospel, and Paul became one of the most articulate early communicators of that mystery. However, the message was not meant to be a secret; the contents were for sharing.

Some communiqués from home countries to their embassies contain information that would be damaging to the host nation if word ever got out. That was the case with the mystery of the gospel; it had huge potential to destabilize the dark, oppressive kingdom of the world. Consequently, Paul was opposed, arrested, and imprisoned. Chained to a Roman soldier, he wrote a letter to the Ephesians. He ended it with an appeal for personal prayer. He did not ask for freedom or comfort. Paul wanted boldness to proclaim the mystery of the gospel as an ambassador of the kingdom of God. Chains would not stop him.

Pray on my behalf, that utterance may be given to me in the opening of my mouth, to make known with boldness the mystery of the gospel, for which I am an ambassador in chains; that in proclaiming it I may speak boldly, as I ought to speak. (Ephesians 6:19–20)

The spiritual geography of the universe is simple. A kingdom of darkness opposes the kingdom of God. Sin gives Satan a grip on lives to trap people in the kingdom of darkness and separate them from God. To complicate things, Satan lies about God, convincing his captives that God is distant, uncaring, or powerless to intervene. From inside Satan's prison camp, any message about God ransoming His people amounted to little more than a mysterious rumor—until Jesus came.

Paul summarized the message in an earlier letter: news about the death, resurrection, and exaltation of Jesus, in fulfillment of Scripture (1 Cor. 15:3–8). Jesus carried that good news (gospel) in His person, explaining and demonstrating the love of God for sinners and His power to break bondages. Christ's crucifixion freed captives from a dead-end life of sin to eternal and abundant life as God's children. People found peace with God.[37]

Anyone who has experienced life on both sides of the border feels compelled to share the good news. It's meant for sharing. It's only a mystery in the sense that Satan hushed it up and that human wisdom cannot grasp it. To receive the message, we need God's illumination, and faith.

But how will anyone hear the message? You and I, like Paul, are heaven's ambassadors. We have grasped the contents of God's communiqué. Let's pray for ourselves and each other to have boldness and clarity as we proclaim the message.

---

37. Ephesians 2:13–18; 6:15; Colossians 1:19–23.

The IN-GROUP

(Parallel: Matthew 11:7–15.)

Jesus had perfect balance when it came to honoring someone. He could bless without flattering; He could give credit to one person without seeming to devalue another in the process. He did it with John the Baptist:

> *What did you go out into the wilderness to look at? ... A prophet?*
> *Yes, I say to you, and one who is more than a prophet. This is the one*
> *about whom it is written, "Behold, I send my messenger before your*
> *face, who will prepare your way before you." I say to you, among those*
> *born of women, there is no one greater than John; yet he who is least*
> *in the kingdom of God is greater than he.* (Luke 7:24–28)

John was greater than the other prophets because he was the messenger foretold by Malachi and he was the direct forerunner of Jesus (Mal. 3:1). The Old Testament prophets had proclaimed the Law and their predecessors' words; John announced the news everyone had been waiting for—the arriving kingdom of God (Luke 16:16). Nonetheless, everyone in the kingdom is greater than him.

Jesus wanted His hearers to understand the greater honor of the "in-group." So, what does it mean to be "in" the kingdom of God? Citizenship in human kingdoms is primarily a birthright; as such, it can never be revoked. The most seditious anarchist might be accommodated in a prison, but they would keep their citizenship. God's kingdom is different; being "in" *depends* on subjection to the King. Becoming His subject begins a relationship with Him, which includes a range of benefits. Our enjoyment of citizenship increases as our relationship with Him grows. There is no such thing as membership by birth, forms, or fees. You can't attend a church on a "tourist visa" and claim citizenship (though you might learn how to become a subject while you visit).

Okay. So, in what ways are citizens greater than John? If we apply the same terms to citizens that Jesus applied to John, then apparently, He considers us greater prophetic messengers of the kingdom. John never experienced the intimacy with the King that Jesus taught and modeled and that we can experience. He had no idea about the cross and resurrection. John issued a press release about the kingdom coming; we have enough backstory, explanation, and experience to make a full-blown documentary.

Entry to the kingdom is marked by pressing through the narrow gate of obedience to God and by double baptism. John had a reputation for the water baptism that washes away the old lifestyle and gives a fresh start, but he could only promise Spirit baptism from Jesus. The Spirit of the risen Jesus fills us and enables us to live like Jesus. The Spirit is His presence; He guides and empowers us to proclaim and demonstrate life in the kingdom, just as Jesus did. We have a greater message and greater power to deliver it.

In-groups are nice when you're in, but painful and irritating when you aren't. Jesus' words were motivational, not restrictive. Everyone can have the great honor of being part of God's kingdom; it only takes submission.

BEING THERE

(Context: Acts 3:1–11; 4:1–22.)

Perhaps we struggle more with what God does not do than with the miracles He does do. Some people ask, "Why, if God is so caring and powerful, does He not remove serious illness from the earth and prevent suffering?" Teachers give many helpful answers, but I suggest it has to do with the core of the kingdom—the King.

For those who accept the possibility of a supreme being engaged with creation, miracles are no stretch. That God tends to limit Himself presents a problem. When the Son of God emptied Himself and became a serving human (Phil. 2:6–7), He took on limitations of time and space. Jesus could only be in one place at one time and only for the length of a truncated lifespan. What's more, He arrived in an era without mass media or hand-held devices for light-speed communication to the other side of the planet.

There's a message in those limitations. When we look closely at the pattern of Jesus' healings, we see that He only did three from a distance at the requests of people who cared deeply about the sick person.[38] Ninety percent happened face to face, usually with one sick person at a time. Forty-five percent included some kind of touch. The pattern suggests that Jesus wanted people to associate miracles with *Him*. They noticed His gentle hands and

---

38. A servant in Matt. 8:5–13, a daughter in Matt. 15:21–28, and a son in John 4:46–54.

the authority in His simple commands. Being there, He could direct glory to God (John 9:3; 11:4, 40). His presence showed the power of heaven flowing from an ordinary-looking man.

Setting aside any presuppositions about how Divinity should behave, Jesus' behavior suggests one thing: His miracles were the result of the Divine presence. Beyond being present, Jesus used no other repeated formula. The powers of darkness submitted to the simple words and touch of Jesus. Miracles demonstrated His royal authority.

"Kingdom" means the rule and reign of a king. To think of the kingdom of God as a system or concept is a sad error. Eventually, it loses its appeal. Kingdom can never be detached from Him. A monarchy is only as strong and good as the monarch who rules over it. Kingdom is not just the *idea* of God's power and compassion; they are in His *nature* and are seen whenever He meets a need.

We see the same pattern with the King's emissaries. Jesus gave authority to His followers to do the same kind of miracles and even greater things (Mark 16:17–18; John 14:12). Having healed the sick, they could say, "The kingdom of God has come near," simply because *they* had come near (Luke 10:9). Kingdom nearness continued after Jesus ascended.

> *As [the religious leaders] observed the confidence of Peter and John, and understood that they were uneducated and untrained men, they were marveling and began to recognize them as having been with Jesus. And seeing the man who had been healed standing with them, they had nothing to say in reply. (Acts 4:13–14)*

All this suggests why God does not simply eradicate sickness. He still does some miracles at a distance, but mostly He wants the glory from healings that are associated with His presence or the presence of His people. The king wants hurting people to feel His caring heart through His subjects. So … He wants us to be there, with them.

WHERE
the RUBBER MEETS
the ROAD

(Context: Acts 3:1–4:31.)

Picture a high-tech car tire designed by state-of-the-art software and drawing on the latest materials science research. Now put the tire on a car, lower the jack, and drive off. That's where the idiom, "where the rubber meets the road," comes from. It's used of any plan, determination, or invention when it is finally applied. It's the moment of truth.

God is supremely confident about His kingdom, but it's harder for His followers. For all the talks we hear about God and His ways, even the stories of other people's experience of kingdom life, nothing can substitute for personal test drives.

Peter and John give us an example of what it looks like when kingdom super-rubber meets the rugged road of life. One afternoon, they strolled to the temple to pray as usual. Sitting in the shade of the massive stone gateway was a lame beggar. He interrupted them with his spiel, and, at that point, they had a choice. Would they revert to instinctive human ways? You know: pretend not to hear, or poke in their pockets for loose change. No. They thought in a new way. Like us, they knew God *could* heal. But, more than that, they knew that God loves to flood gaping holes of human need with kingdom wholeness and provision.

Peter, along with John, fixed his gaze upon [the lame man] and said,
"Look at us!" And he began to give them his attention, expecting to
receive something from them. But Peter said, "I do not possess silver
and gold, but what I do have I give to you: In the name of Jesus Christ
the Nazarene—walk!" (Acts 3:4–6)

It happened. Peter helped the man to his feet. They became strong, and the man began walking, leaping, and praising God.

The pair faced two other road tests right away. First, the crowds on their way to prayer time began to gather around in amazement. Oh how we humans like having the power to attract attention and become something of a celebrity. We probably all exploit it at least a tiny bit. The disciples did not. Peter spoke out again. The miracle had happened by faith in Jesus, not by their power or piety. He pointed to God's plan for Jesus to die and be raised, and called on the people to repent and receive Jesus. Five thousand did (Acts 3:11–26; 4:4).

Second, the religious police arrested them. At their trial, they could have cowered and blabbered like so many of us when we are cornered. Instead, empowered by the Spirit, they stuck to the same message about Jesus (Acts 4:1–12). When the leaders warned them never to publicize Jesus' name again, they might have taken the opportunity to submit and be grateful for a merciful release. However, they were defiant: "Whether it is right in the sight of God to give heed to you rather than to God, you be the judge; for we cannot stop speaking what we have seen and heard" (Acts 4:19–20). They returned to the other disciples. All of them ignored the threats and prayed for confidence—and more miracles (Acts 4:23–31).

Peter and John did not swerve because of the pressures. They thought and responded in kingdom ways. Everyone else was behaving in the typical human ways. The lame man saw Peter and John as a potential source of coins. The amazed crowd thought they were miracle-working superstars. The ever-suspicious authorities simply tried to prevent disruptive news from spreading.

What happens to our understanding of God's kingdom when it meets the hard road of our lives? You know: the doctor's frown; the machine that spits back your bank card with a blunt message, "Insufficient funds;" unpleasant people; interruptions; so much left to do on Saturday evening that sabbath seems a waste; the slap in the face delivered in a termination letter. What about the homeless and the hurting that sleep in the shade of our city stores, or those who are confused about and questioning even the basics of life? What will we do next time we hear someone express a need?

Kingdom rubber is excellent. But do we trust it deeply enough to drive on it? If we need to ask the Holy Spirit to clarify the truth about the kingdom to us, let's do that quickly. Then, let's take every opportunity to release the kingdom into the situations we encounter, just as the first disciples did. All it took was simple commands and actions—just like Jesus and His first followers.

The
BLUE TOUCH PAPER

(Context: Matthew 8:1–17, 23–34; 9:1–8. Parallels: Mark 1:29–2:12; 4:35–5:20
Luke 4:38–41; 5:12–26; 7:1–10; 8:22–39.)

It was a simple job with spectacular results. I had a lot of fun that evening. The organizer had asked me to light the fuses on the fireworks for a local display. They each came with one instruction emblazoned in appropriate red or yellow: "Light the blue touch paper and stand back."

Matthew's account of Jesus' ministry immediately after the Sermon on the Mount reads like a firework display of miracles. The multitudes that had marveled at His authoritative teaching followed Him and saw the practical extent of that authority. Right there, at the foot of the mountain, *a leper came to Him, and bowed down to Him, saying, "Lord, if You are willing, You can make me clean." And He stretched out His hand and touched him, saying, "I am willing; be cleansed."* (Matthew 8:2–3)

Jesus' words acted like a flame to a short fuse. Cleansed skin spread over the leper's body like the sparks of an exploding rocket. Whoosh!

Leaving the leper to formalize his cure with a local priest, Jesus headed home to Capernaum. There, a centurion implored Him to heal his paralyzed servant. The officer understood authority. He told the great physician that he didn't need a home visit. "Just say the word." Boom! Within the hour, the servant was up again.

At Peter's house, Jesus touched the hand of His sickly hostess as though it was blue touch paper. Pow! She hopped out of bed, healthy again, eager to serve snacks.

Caught in a sudden violent storm on a boat trip across Galilee, Jesus demonstrated bold faith by rebuking the winds and waves with dramatic effect.

On the eastern shore of Galilee, Jesus and His disciples encountered violent demoniacs. A single word, "Begone!" was enough to dispatch the demons. Poooff!

Back in Capernaum, stretcher-bearers delivered a paralytic to Him. Unlike the case of the centurion's servant, Jesus mixed in a dose of forgiveness to free nerves, joints, and bones from their immobility. Fizzz!

On and on went the show. What were the fireworks for? They marked the arrival of the kingdom of heaven on earth. The boundaries of darkness retreated as Jesus toured Galilee during those days. Each miracle lit up another dark corner of the heavenly places: leprosy, for so long untouchable, was vanquished; paralysis loosened; intimidating demons driven from their territory; the untamable forces of water and air conquered. Women and despised leaders of a foreign occupying force became welcome beneficiaries of God's merciful healing. Even sin, which had dragged its victim incapacitated onto his bed, loosed its hold at Jesus' word. The kingdom of God broke through all barriers.

I hear someone saying, "But that was Jesus, the Son of God. We're different." Remember, the Spirit of the risen Jesus is given to us to live the same way as He did. For Jesus, miracles were part of everyday life. For us, the heirs of the kingdom, the challenge is to exercise our God-given kingdom authority with commands or actions whenever we see a need or an opportunity.

It's simple and fun, just like lighting the blue touch paper.

ABOUT
the AUTHOR

John Avery is the author of *The Name Quest: Explore the Names of God to Grow in Faith and Get to Know Him Better* (Morgan James Publishing, 2015). *The Name Quest* won the 2016 Oregon Christian Writers' Cascade Award for nonfiction. A compilation of short pieces, *The Questions of Jesus*, was published in 2022.

John is a trained teacher with over thirty years' experience as a Bible teaching pastor, small group leader, missionary, and disciple maker. He has lived in England, Israel, Africa, and the Caribbean, ministering with Youth With A Mission (YWAM), international student ministry, and local churches. He and his wife, Janet, now make their home in Oregon. John likes to hike, snowshoe, and cross-country ski. John writes short, thought-provoking Bible devotionals at *www.BibleMaturity.com* many of which will be compiled into books like this one. He maintains a comprehensive resource for all the names of God at *www.NamesForGod.net*.

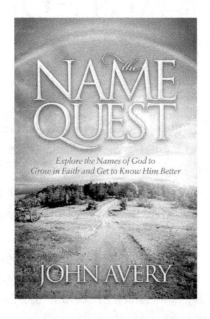

**Watch for future compilations
in the Sparks Series on topics like:**

The Questions of Jesus
(Published October 2022)

Our Identity as Children of God

Talking to God

Faith in God

The Spirit of God

Following the Voice of God

Revival from God

Prophets of God

Names of God

Followers of Jesus

Kings of Israel
(David, Saul, and others)

Fathers of Faith
(Abraham, Jacob, and Moses)

Various other in-depth devotionals are at
www.BibleMaturity.com

THE SPARKS SERIES

CPSIA information can be obtained
at www.ICGtesting.com
Printed in the USA
JSHW010401090123
35931JS00005B/24

9 780998 650760